The Epic of Gilgamesh

THE EPIC OF GILGAMESH

"Then fortune smiled so fully on my acts
    that I began, at 3:00 a.m. beneath a swollen
moon,
to intone an epic, being first antiphonarion once
    again, as I'd been when a boy in noble,
holy woods surrounded by my brothers
    and sure that God had callen me
to speak for Him."

DEDICATION

for Bak Shar
whose death gave birth
to this

The Epic of Gilgamesh

Verse rendition by
Danny P. Jackson

Introduction by
Robert D. Biggs

Illustrated by
Thom Kapheim

BOLCHAZY-CARDUCCI PUBLISHERS

Typography:

Bratislava, Slovakia

Design: Tibor Hrabovský
General Editor: Georgine Grek Cooper

©Copyright 1992
BOLCHAZY-CARDUCCI PUBLISHERS
1000 Brown Street
Wauconda, Illinois 60084

Printed in the United States of America

Original printing 1992
Last figure below indicates year of this printing:
99   98   97   96   95   94   93

International Standard Book Number:
Hardbound 0-86516-251-4
Softbound 0-86516-252-2
Student Edition 0-86516-250-6

Library of Congress Cataloging-in-Publication Data

Gilgamesh. English.
    The epic of Gilgamesh / verse rendition by Danny P.
Jackson : introduction by Robert D. Biggs : illustrated by Thom
Kapheim.
            p.   cm.
    Translation of: Gilgamesh.
    Includes bibliographical references and index.
    ISBN 0-86516-251-4 : $35.00. – ISBN 0-86516-252-2 :
$15.00. – ISBN 0-86516-250-6 (student ed.) : $4.95
    I. Jackson, Danny P., 1946-   II. Title.
    PJ3771.G5E5   1992
    892'.1–dc20
                                                    92-8189
                                                    CIP

TABLE OF CONTENTS

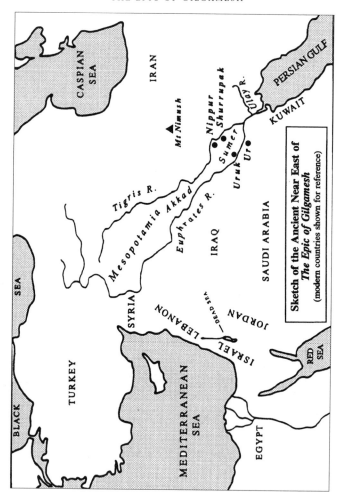

Sketch of the Ancient Near East of
The Epic of Gilgamesh
(modern countries shown for reference)

LIST OF ILLUSTRATIONS
From the Ancient World

Figure

Original Artwork by Thom Kapheim

PUBLISHER'S PREFACE

Why publish The Epic of Gilgamesh?

I first learned of the *Gilgamesh* in 1967 at the State University of New York at Albany while working on a doctorate in classics. It was Berkeley Peabody, chairman of the comparative literature department, who casually mentioned the *Gilgamesh* to me.

As a practicing Catholic and a former seminarian, I wondered why I hadn't been told that, long before recorded Judeo-Christian literature and doctrine, ancient cultures told the same stories pondering the same human condition: Adam and Eve, Paradise Lost and the Great Flood came to life in the tablets of the epic in haunting similarity to the Biblical accounts.

I was fascinated with the work, this first extant epic, this first hero, this first set of mythical parallels to — in fact, a predecessor of — the Bible.

As a man, I could empathize with Gilgamesh on his journey through the various stages of coming of age and rites of passage: the unbridled libido gradually yielding to the social drive to produce something of fame; the eventual realization that one does not find satisfaction in pursuit of self-satisfaction, that in a mature relationship a new whole is born of two and is richer and deeper than either one; bereavement giving birth to sheer terror of one's own mortality; wasted aerobics of the body and soul aimed at foiling the grim reaper — even if only for a couple more years; finally, resignation and the mustering of courage to accept the limitations of one's nature, making the best of the opportunities here and now without any expectations beyond this life. All of these are mapped out along the road that Gilgamesh must follow.

Why a New Edition ?

I have taught the epic at every opportunity in such courses as the epic and mythology. Yet I felt the available texts to be inadequate. While some were accurate in scholarship, the obtrusive lacunae and notations posed problems with readability, dampening the interest of the students. Others provided a smoother flowing prose rendition, but lacked the poetic grandeur that is so vital an element of the epic.

This fascinating tale, so significant to Western thought, deserves a beautifully poetic, *readable* presentation that will capture the interest and provoke the minds of our students.

Ladislaus J. Bolchazy, Ph.D.

INTRODUCTION

I welcome this edition of *The Epic of Gilgamesh* for making accessible to modern readers the poetry and the drama, presented in heroic terms, of life, love, friendship, and finally, the recognition of the ultimate reality of human existence. It is one of the great epic tales surviving from the ancient world of The-Land-Between-The-Two-Rivers, Mesopotamia, and though incomplete, reflects an ancient range of human experience and emotion not so far removed from our own.

The literary background of this epic is complex, and the version from King Ashurbanipal's library in the Assyrian capital of Nineveh is the culmination of a literary tradition covering many hundreds of years—in fact, more than a thousand. The story apparently had great appeal in the ancient world, for fragments of versions are known far beyond the confines of ancient Mesopotamia—in Hittite and Hurrian from Anatolia, and in Elamite from Armavir-blur in Armenia.

There exist a number of translations into various languages from the original Babylonian and Assyrian tablets—and for their Sumerian forerunners for some episodes. Other renditions—some more literal than others, some more poetic than others—have been created by using the ancient cuneiform text as a basis. I readily recognize that many previous editions are frustratingly philological in their interpretation and typographically ugly, with numerous lacunae and their areas of italics to indicate uncertain translations. While Dan Jackson's edition is not as literal as some, he captures the spirit of this universal tale. Jackson chooses not to be encumbered by philological disputes and broken passages. He has woven the surviving text into a full-bodied epic, using the format of the ancient, six-column cuneiform tablets.

The epic states, "When the gods created mankind, they allotted death to mankind, keeping life eternal for themselves." Yet while mortality is inevitable, Jackson's lyrical and moving presentation gives renewed life to this wonderful tale of Gilgamesh.

Robert D. Biggs
The Oriental Institute
of The University of Chicago

December, 1991

ILLUSTRATIONS

The photographs on the pages that follow represent the ancient world and have been included to establish an historical context for the epic while building a bridge to modern understanding. Among them are objects not only from the era thought to include the reign of Gilgamesh the king, but objects suggesting the evolution and synthesis of tales of Gilgamesh the mythical hero into a variety of later cultures.

The captions by Robert D. Biggs outline the background of objects that reflect aspects of literature, daily life and religion. Figures 1 and 2 suggest the beginnings of the literary tradition. Figures 3-5 may provide insight into "a day in the life of" the ancient Mesopotamian in the cradle of civilization and a connection to the modern world of that same area, where similar boats and reed huts are in use today. Figures 6-10 imply the prominence of religion in the lives of the ancients. Intricately constructed ziggurats (temple-towers) and finely crafted religious statues survive as a testament to the importance of religious activity. Finally, figures 11-18 perhaps glorify and immortalize the exploits of mythical heroes in mediums ranging from vase and vessel to architecture. A prominence and universality among cultures of the art and enjoyment of storytelling is suggested.

Figures 19-33, found among the pages of the text, are from the series of original works of art by Thom Kapheim, commissioned by the publisher and designed to tell the tale in pictures. These fifteen prints from hand-carved woodcuts reflect the heroic richness and depth of an individual's attempt to define and exceed the boundaries of the world outlined by his human and religious experience.

Photograph of a fragment of Tablet XI, the "Flood Tablet" of *The Epic of Gilgamesh*, inscribed in Assyrian cuneiform characters. (figure 1)

Head of the Assyrian king Ashurbanipal, 669-627 B.C., a detail of a limestone panel. The excavations of his library provided a major source of Mesopotamian literature, including a good portion of *The Epic of Gilgamesh*. (figure 2)

Relief decoration on a stone trough of about 1900 B.C., depicting a traditional reed house. Dwellings constructed of such bundles of reeds are still being made and occupied in the marsh areas of southern Iraq. (figure 3)

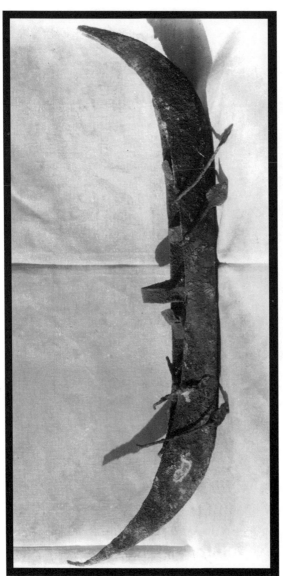

An ancient miniature boat from Ur of a type Gilgamesh might have used on his voyage to seek Utnapishtim. Such model boats, usually of baked clay, are often found in excavations in southern Iraq. The shape is identical to the *tarada*, the kind of boat that is even today propelled in the shallow waters of the marshes by paddles or punting poles. (figure 4)

A gypsum plaque, about 2700-2600 B.C., depicting a man and woman at a banquet, while servants bring food and drink, and musicians and dancers perform. It is believed that the hole in the center was for a peg which helped to secure doors.

(figure 5)

Ziggurat at the Eanna sanctuary at Warka, ancient Uruk, in southern Iraq. (figure 6)

The ziggurat at Ur during excavations in the 1930s. It was extensively restored by the Iraqi Department of Antiquities in the 1960s, but was reportedly damaged in the 1991 war. (figure 7)

Artist's drawing of a suggested reconstruction of the temple tower (ziggurat) of the Sumerian king Ur-Nammu, about 2100 B.C., at the ancient city of Ur. The Tower of Babel in the Bible was likely such a structure. (figure 8)

Copper representation of four-faced god with foot on a crouching ram
and goddess holding a vase, from Ishchali, Iraq, about 18th to 17th
century B.C.
(figure 9)

Sumerian stone statuette, about 2900-2600 B.C. Such statuettes are believed to represent a worshipper standing in a prayerful attitude before his god in a temple. Stone was very scarce in ancient Mesopotamia, so such statues were very expensive gifts to the deity. (figure 10)

Stone relief from Tell Halaf, about 1000 B.C., perhaps depicting
Gilgamesh and Enkidu's battle with Humbaba.
(figure 11)

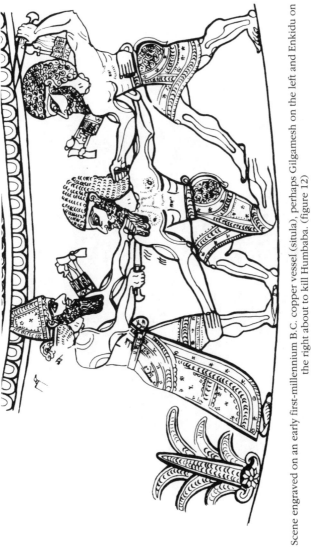

Scene engraved on an early first-millennium B.C. copper vessel (situla), perhaps Gilgamesh on the left and Enkidu on the right about to kill Humbaba. (figure 12)

This modern rolling of a cylinder seal in the Assyrian style of the early first millennium B.C. may depict the killing of Humbaba. (figure 13)

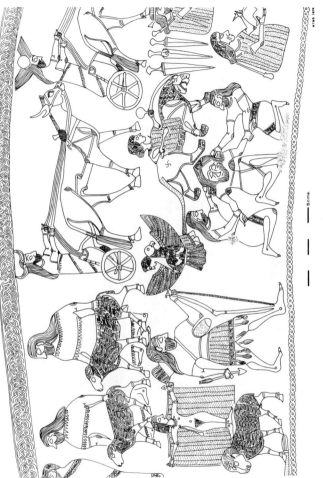

The two men attacking the figure between them, depicted on this gold bowl (in the lower right area) from Hasanlu, Iran, may represent Gilgamesh and Enkidu. (figure 14)

The central group in this rolling of an Assyrian seal of about 750-650 B.C. may show the monster Humbaba being attacked. (figure 15)

Copper double vase, each vase balanced on the head of a male wrestler, third millennium B.C. It has occasionally been suggested that such scenes represent the first meeting of Gilgamesh and Enkidu as they vie with each other.
(figure 16)

This rolling of a cylinder seal of the late third millennium B.C. shows on the left a nude hero subduing a bull. It does not necessarily represent Gilgamesh attacking the Bull of Heaven, though this has been suggested. (figure 17)

Cylinder seal impression with hero subduing a bull, similar to the preceding one, from the third quarter of the third millennium B.C. (figure 18)

UNDERSTANDING THIS EDITION

Overview

When I first taught this book as part of an introductory course at the City University of New York, it was used to entice students and to provide them with something that none of the other classics offered. Its simplicity, directness and freshness made *The Epic of Gilgamesh* unique and outstanding among the other ancient masterpieces we studied. Naturally, it was taught first since it is chronologically the oldest of our Western writings. It was also a great choice as a curtain raiser for another reason. Much of its charm and success stem from the fact that it is so basic a story, so promising an overture. "When you read, you begin with A, B, C," and "when you sing, you begin with do, re, mi." It's like that with the world of literature, and for this reason *The Epic of Gilgamesh* is the best opening song for courses because it is so fundamental and so likely to please many students without intimidating them.

Understandably enough, the contents and context of the work need to be explained properly for a generation sometimes criticized for not having the historical knowledge to enjoy the story. Like some other myths, *The Epic of Gilgamesh* celebrates a hero whose life and death are special. Other epic heroes, like Beowulf, Cuchulainn, Achilles, Roland or Leopold Bloom, had their stories told by master mythmakers because their lives were either extraordinary in ordinary times or ordinary in extraordinary times. Authors like Greece's Homer or Ireland's Joyce shaped classic or modern myths for reasons that cannot be explained briefly. When oral traditions in countries like France or Ireland produce epics through the generational efforts of several poets, the final product is often singularly beautiful for those who share the language and ethos of the clan, but either partially or totally incomprehensible to foreigners.

The passions and pathos of the character of Gilgamesh, however, have universal appeal. The song of his exploits is simple and challenging, unadorned but varied. Never mind that the fragmentary tablets are incomplete and sometimes disjointed. Never mind that experts disagree on anything from pronunciation to interpretation. What has survived the sands and centuries is a tale both lusty and tender that retains the ability to arouse compassion and empathy in all who join Gilgamesh on his journey.

The Story

The plot is fairly simple. Gilgamesh is a great hero who dominates the ancient Sumerian city of Uruk during the third millennium B.C. Unchallenged by any rival, he lords it over one and all until his subjects, weary of his arrogance and indiscriminate exercise of power, ask the gods to divert his impetuous ways by creating a suitable rival to keep him busy. An appropriate comrade is fashioned in the form of Enkidu, a warrior as skilled as Gilgamesh, who becomes his boon companion or other self after an initial rite of challenge. Their shared adventures and exploits forge a strong and intimate bond between them. But a vengeful god, infuriated by their combined assault, engineers a tragic outcome for their friendship. Enkidu's fate is inevitable, and Gilgamesh is forced to reconsider many things previously taken for granted. His sense of joy is shattered by that most complicated of emotions: grief. His interest in civic duty, in pleasure, in the divine, in his appearance and in all other matters is changed profoundly. Because of the crisis in faith that he experiences, Gilgamesh's world view is altered permanently. As a result, he wanders and wonders. Tested, tormented and tried by fate, he finally arrives at a new understanding of himself and of our place in the cosmic order of life. His bravado is now mingled with tears.

The results startle many a modern reader expecting the characters of ancient literature to have no more emotional or perceptual depth than the cave paintings of antiquity. The Gilgamesh who survives this story, kind reader, perceives much the same reality as you when, fresh from your journey of dreams, you peer into your morning mirror. Forlorn, refreshed, expectant, informed and all-too-human, Gilgamesh's face by the end of the epic is as multifaceted as his mind. Something miraculous has happened. Experience has forced the immature braggart to redefine his idea of the holy. His dark night of the soul is behind him. A terrible beauty has been born.

The Approach

There are many questions about the epic that remain unanswered. Since it is the oldest text in Western literature and comes from a Near Eastern milieu that is as remote for certain students as another galaxy, the problems arise quickly. They are hard to address. When investigating Dante, for example, teachers often exploit what students already know about Vergil or Christianity. When students deal first with Vergil, they can rely on whatever is already known about Homeric precedents that form the *Aeneid*. In the case of Gilgamesh, this cannot be done, as no earlier models or allusions exist.

For some readers, the story becomes as dry and deadly as the sands from which the tablets were extracted. For others, however, just the opposite is true. The archaeologist-in-us-all warms to an investigation of our literary origins. Indeed, it was sufficient for me in class back in 1974 to say only that the fragments on which the original text was inscribed were found at a site not unlike the one shown at the start of the first *Exorcist* movie. Eyes widened immediately. Hands were raised for questions. And so the fun began. I didn't even have to stoop to explaining the curse that haunts those who handle the treasure improperly.

In teaching the epic at the beginning of survey courses, I used to make the mistake of saying that it was a good start, but that what would follow in the works of Vergil and Dante would provide the real fireworks of a grand finale concluding with the epics of Joyce and Kazantzakis. I realize now that I was wrong, and I fervently hope that the next generation of scholars will not take as long to see that such a Eurocentric approach to world literature is crippling. Please keep in mind that Athens and Jerusalem and Rome are only the widely publicized centers of ancient thought. What happened in Nineveh, Ch'ang-an and Emain Macha is as valid and worthwhile as anything that Londoners wrote centuries later.

Interpretation

What, then, you may ask, does all this mean?

I shall leave the interpretation of such matters to those women and men, teachers of students, who use this text in courses here and there. As one who taught for twenty years, beginning at a kindergarten in the South Bronx, I remain humbly respectful of the burdens of educators. Even the simplest of fairy tales can have mixed meanings. This epic, as complex and deep as it is plain and straightforward, is an enigma. And, like other puzzles, *The Epic of Gilgamesh* enthralls us because it is so fresh, so heart-rending and so mesmerizing even while it remains problematically a part of an ancient intrigue.

If you're new at this and lack the historical or

linguistic background needed to enjoy a song so inviting on your first reading, do not despair. Give the words a chance to work a little magic in your heart and dreams. Later, your mind will follow, and you can join the ranks of those who never lose their wonder for lightning or for thunder, for fog or for books that contain flash and boom as well as solemnity and mystery.

Those of you who have some faith, who are already predisposed to be comfortable with a character who sheds his lustiness and displays a profound and beautiful spirituality, have some advantage. If you have reflected on God, you will stay with Gilgamesh as he does the same. If you have ever been tempted to abandon your own faith, it will be easy to feel as Gilgamesh does when he faces that same possibility. Lastly, if you have ever cried yourself to sleep (as perhaps we all should sometimes do), then your heart will be sensitized while learning of one beset by woe at the loss of his friend.

The universality of such sentiments may, in fact, explain why the epic has received wide recognition and the frequent attention of translators since its relatively recent re-discovery. Students around the world are now reading versions of this epic because the story contains obvious, frequent and fascinating parallels to other eras and literature. Specialists in the field of theology have followed the lead of Alexander Heidel by continuing to trace counterparts in Biblical works. Some links, like the flood account, can be clearly delineated. Others beg for comparison, like the thematic similarities between this epic and the Old Testament (paradise lost, Adam's seduction by Eve, and the encounter with mortality). And still other issues, like the one of how we perceive the sexual protocol of pagan religions, cannot yet be treated well.

As you read and consider these matters, keep in mind that the story itself has not been completely retrieved from the ruins discovered in the last century amid the archaeological sites of the Near East. The twelve tablets we possess are in fragments. While international scholarship today continues to improve our collective efforts, experts in Japan and Czecho-Slovakia do not all agree on the poetic, linguistic, religious and historical meaning of the epic. Computers have enabled us to learn some things that could not be traced thirty years ago. But the lack of cooperation on the part of different nationalities makes it, unfortunately, impossible for current knowledge to be quickly exchanged. Saddest of all, the turmoil of war ravages and re-ravages the landscape on which this story was enacted so long ago. A glance at the map will show the informed reader how the places in the epic coincide with locations in the modern world that are so often stained by the blood and tears of men, women and children.

The Translation

Like other renditions or re-workings, this one was influenced by various models. I studied with Allen Mandelbaum and Frederick Goldin while at the Graduate Center of the City University of New York and then taught classics with James Mantinband at Brooklyn College. Their translations of Vergil, Dante, *The Song of Roland* and Lucretius impressed me a great deal. Recent conversations with Philip Fried, editor of *The Manhattan Review,* were also extremely helpful.

My fellow classicists should accept this as one of many attempts being made in our time to resuscitate an interest in various disciplines. My primary intent was poetic. No efforts were made to remind historians of the intentionally provocative re-creations that Ezra Pound used to make his *Homage to Sextus Propertius* as famous as it justly is. Nor would I welcome for this *Gilgamesh* the kind of brouhaha that surrounded the reception of Pound's "translation."

Most of what you'll find here will be easily recognized. It can be compared fairly to the other fine renditions of this epic published in the last three decades. When I have embellished the text with what may seem like Broadway lyrics, hymns or the linguistic echoes of *Weltschmerz*, it was because I sensed a dimension to the text that was previously ignored. I commenced and concluded by attempting to translate the spirit rather than the word.

In harmony with my commitment to the spirit of the tale, I have avoided use of words like harlot or prostitute to describe Shamhat, the woman who brought civilization to Enkidu. Such terms are used almost universally in other translations and references to the epic, and they indeed represent a literal translation of the word. She was not, however, what we understand such terms to mean. We have no modern counterpart to, or context within which to understand, the sacred nature of her role. An understanding of the ancient culture within which she existed would clear up any misconceptions about her moral stature. Since the first-time reader of the epic very probably lacks this understanding, I feel that my terminology simplifies matters and projects a more accurate image.

Regardless of how specialists receive this version, I remain confident that general readers will appreciate the collective effort made here to provide a new generation with the most attractive rendition of Gilgamesh available in English.

Historical Note

The area of the world known to American students as the Near East has a rich and varied history. Current disputes over the boundaries of countries now sharing the region (Iraq, Iran and Kuwait) notwithstanding, there exists a regional heritage that stretches back to ancestors whose greatness pre-dated Muhammad and Jesus by thousands of years. Indeed, an oral and written story-telling tradition much older than the earliest Biblical books of the Jewish scriptures flourished in ancient Mesopotamia, one of the settings of this epic.

A little over 100 years ago we discovered records of some ancient Near Eastern kingdoms at towns like Babylon, Ur and Nineveh. Time has combined with chance and war to destroy much of the writing produced by citizens using the Sumerian, Akkadian and Hittite languages. (Even the ancient Greeks seem to have known little about these vast, powerful civilizations, although the philosopher Aelian [ca. A.D. 170-235] includes reference to a Gilgamos character in his writings.) But the efforts of these lost people to memorialize their stories by inscribing them on clay tablets were impressive. Such activities were a serious, possibly sacred, undertaking. Because of work by scribes like Sin-Leqi-Unninni, the ancient name most often credited with the care and editing of *The Epic of Gilgamesh,* we have been able to gain rare insights into our origins.

Of all the artifacts retrieved from archaeological sites, none has caused greater excitement among literary specialists than this book. It tells the story of Gilgamesh, a king in the town of Uruk who lived a fantastic life sometime around 2700 B.C. Centuries later, the first written accounts of his exploits were recorded. These probably recalled some of the experiences attributed to him by admirers who mixed myth with history to celebrate the greatness of a legendary ruler.

While his accomplishments were impressive and recorded within his own vicinity, the epic that heralded his greatness seems to have had limited popularity in the immediate area of Uruk itself. By the time the stories were repeated, revised and written on the tablets for safekeeping at Ashurbanipal's library (ca. 700 B.C.), counterparts existed that have been found at Megiddo (Palestine), Boghazkoy (Turkey) and Ugarit (Syria). These duplications prompt some to think that the epic was much admired and almost certainly recognized

enough to influence later writings, like the Book of
Genesis, which also dealt with the themes of flood,
death, and the quest for immortality.

The nineteenth century discovery of the epic raised
three names high in the archaeological Hall of Fame:
Austen Henry Layard, Hormuzd Rassam and George
Smith. Their efforts brought the world's attention to the
existence and significance of the story. The publicity
that accompanied their work changed popular thinking
about antiquity.

Born in 1817, Austen Henry Layard was a Frenchman
who became an English diplomat and led British
expeditions into the Near East as Undersecretary of
Foreign Affairs. His unending curiosity about
Mesopotamia led him to unearth the palace library of
Ashurbanipal at Nineveh during the 1860s where his
workers found numerous significant artifacts.

When Layard left the site, the search continued, and
the tablets on which the epic is inscribed were found by
Hormuzd Rassam, a native of the area employed as an
interpreter and jack-of-all-trades. Prior to these
excavations, Rassam spent two years imprisoned by King
Theodore of Abyssinia. After his release, he began the
mound digging of a temple eight miles north of Nimrud
at Balawat and in 1866 located there the tablets which
would then be sent to London for deciphering.

The act of translating these inscriptions, so cryptically
fashioned in a manner to which classicists were not
accustomed, involved George Smith. An engraver and a
self-taught, amateur Assyriologist, Smith was an eccentric
who was devoted to the interpretation of antiquities.
Through the early 1870s, he pored over the fragmented
tablets and rendered their eleven sections into what was
a total revelation. No one had ever before suggested
that Assyric-Babylonian literature contained anything as
old or as rich as this. Excitedly, Smith won publicity that
helped fund his own personal search for another 384
fragmented clay tablets which contained the missing

parts of the controversial myth of Utnapishtim. This predecessor of Noah is the protagonist of a flood-survivor story that rocked Victorian England because of the challenge it made to accounts given in what was believed to be an incontestable version of creation.

Smith's bombshell coincided with breathtaking announcements from other fields of study and helped to shape modern thinking. It inspired debate, as did the theories of secular or religious thinkers like Darwin, Mendel, Nietzsche and Kierkegaard. The breakthroughs represented by the work of these individuals pushed scholars and editors toward a new century with intoxicating speed while the nations of Europe hurled armies at each other with unprecedented ferocity. It is no wonder that this epic, so concerned with the death struggle called *agon* by the Greeks, speaks to us so clearly in this century. While its influence in antiquity was limited, it can be argued that *The Epic of Gilgamesh* has become a particularly significant document about life for the twentieth century, one which has verifiably changed the way modernity views its relation with the past.

But recognition for the great age of its tablets or the uniqueness of its place in literary history did not keep the epic from various forms of abuse. Editors and publishers have sometimes been forced to present it in textbook type excerpts that have added to a misunderstanding of the story. Translators themselves, capable of reflecting those cultural prejudices that soil legitimate scholarship, have also rendered the original in a way that adds to the debate over the theology, politics and sexual behavior of the ancient world. Indeed, the treatment of the discovered tablets themselves arouses another type of controversy. The scattering around the world of such relics incites debate. Fragments of the tablets found in the 1860s, bought and sold legitimately or pirated, are displayed in museums that are now accused of exploiting what they claim to cherish. Like contemporary Athenians who petition the British annually for the return of the marbles from the Acropolis, there are citizens who believe that what was found at Nineveh should have stayed there. That controversy may be as important a part of the epic's fate as any that centers on exegesis.

Despite such treatment by the well-intentioned, the epic has had its share of devoted experts who have worked to shepherd it toward another century of existence. None of those sponsors worked more diligently than Alexander Heidel who, laboring at The Oriental Institute of The University of Chicago, produced in 1946 a title invaluable to all later work in English on this subject. His *The Gilgamesh Epic and Old Testament Parallels* is a companion to his monograph *The Babylonian Genesis,* and it presented the best current thinking on the mythic, religious and historical issues related to the epic. His translation, originally intended for the Assyrian Dictionary files of the Oriental Institute, has been criticized as circumspect and unpoetic by those who fail to appreciate his scholarly objective. There is absolute need for such caution in dealing with what will become a prototype for a work from another language. If no poet ever respects for long what sounds archaic, then it is no wonder that each generation tries to find a new voice for old songs. But poetic taste caters to popular fashion just as the painstaking protocol of exegesis is dictated by sound scholarship. There may be no good reason for believing that the two are mutually exclusive, but the *explication de texte* calls for considerations that have nothing to do with the beauty of words. And what Alexander Heidel did allowed many translators to try something with Gilgamesh that they would not have had a chance to do without him.

In addition to Heidel's work, there are several editions of the epic available for consultation. They differ in ambition, intent and degree of success. No evaluation of their merits is appropriate here, but readers of this presentation can supplement their knowledge of translation by consulting any of the following:

1. *The Epic of Gilgamesh,* R. Campbell Thompson, Clarendon, 1930.
2. *The Epic of Gilgamesh,* N.K. Sandars, Penguin, 1960.
3. *Gilgamesh A Verse Narrative,* Herbert Mason, New American Library, 1970.
4. *Gilgamesh,* John Gardner and John Maier, Vintage, 1985.
5. *The Epic of Gilgamesh,* Maureen Kovacs, Stanford, 1985.

As for the scholarship that an undergraduate might appreciate on the epic and its context, students can benefit from the following in different ways.

1. *Gods, Graves, and Scholars: The Story of Archaeology,* C.W. Ceram, Vintage, 1951.
2. *Ancient Mesopotamia Portrait of a Dead Civilization,* A. Leo Oppenheim, Universtiy of Chicago Press, 1964.
3. *The Evolution of the Gilgamesh Epic,* Jeffrey H. Tigay, University of Pennsylvania, 1983.
4. *The Gilgamesh Epic and Old Testament Parallels,* Alexander Heidel, University of Chicago, 1946.
5. *The Story of Civilization, Vol. 1 Our Oriental Heritage,* Will Durant, Simon and Schuster, 1935.
6. *Myths from Mesopotamia Creation, the Flood, Gilgamesh, and Others,* Stephanie Dalley, Oxford University Press, 1991.

Acknowledgments

Credit is due here to Dena Justin and Bernard Dick who taught me to render the thought as well as the word while introducing me to Greek at Iona College. My students, especially Peter Gelman, Dennis Gonya and Jacquie Battle, as well as my own children, Dan and Cara, and my wife Lorraine have guided my hand in yet another way. Special tribute is due to my father, not only for teaching me to read, but for having been the gentlest of Irish storytellers.

Lastly, I cannot forget the many wonderful neighbors whose many wonderful accents delighted my ears for the thirty years I lived among them in the Bronx.

Give them all some credit. I take whatever blame is deserved. And blame may well be mine, for no explanation of this "translation" will satisfy certain critics. And there is no chance here for a lengthy treatment of the art of translation or the perennial issues involved in such matters.

The New Jersey Shore   Danny P. Jackson
Christmas Eve, 1990

Main Characters of the Epic

Gilgamesh, the hero and king of Uruk

Enkidu, his new friend

Ninsun, wise goddess and mother of Gilgamesh

Shamhat, sacred girl who brought the two friends together

Anu, father of the gods and patron of Uruk

Humbaba, monster god who must be killed

Ishtar, the king's spurned and vengeful suitor-goddess

Enlil, god who unleashes the great flood

Siduri, the barmaid with worldly advice

Urshanabi, the boatman who gives passage to paradise

Utnapishtim, who holds the secret of eternal life

who hoards the girls of other men
for his own purpose
(figure 19)

Tablet I

Columns i - vi

Gilgamesh, the King

The Creation of Enkidu

The Civilization of Enkidu

Gilgamesh Dreams of Enkidu

TABLET I

Column i

Fame haunts the man who visits Hell,
who lives to tell my entire tale identically.
So like a sage, a trickster or saint,
GILGAMESH
was a hero who knew secrets and saw
forbidden places,
who could even speak of the time before the
Flood because he lived long, learned much,
and spoke his life to those who first
cut into clay his bird-like words.
10 He commanded walls for Uruk and for Eanna,
our holy ground,
walls that you can see still; walls where weep
the weary widows of dead soldiers.
Go to them and touch their immovable presence
with gentle finger to find yourself.
No one else ever built such walls.
Climb Uruk's Tower and walk about on a
windy night. Look. Touch. Taste. Sense.
What force creates such mass?
20 Open up the special box that's hidden in the wall
and read aloud the story of Gilgamesh's life.
Learn what sorrow taught him; learn of those
he overcame by wit or force or fear as he,
a town's best child, acted nobly in the way
one should to lead and acted wisely too
as one who sought no fame.
Child of Lugalbanda's wife and some great force,
Gilgamesh is a fate alive, the
finest babe of Ninsun, she who never
30 let a man touch her, indeed
so pure and heavenly, so without sin.
He knew the secret paths that reached the eagle's
nest above the mountain and he knew too how
just to drop a well into the chilly earth.

He sailed the sea to where Shamash comes,
explored the world, sought life, and came at last
to Utnapishtim far away who did bring
back to life the flooded earth.
Is there anywhere a greater king
40 who can say, as Gilgamesh may,
"I am supreme"?

Column ii

The bigger part of him was made in heaven
and the smaller part somewhere on earth.
She-who-must-be-obeyed fashioned his body's self.
She endowed him.
Gilgamesh watches the flocks of Uruk himself
as if he were a loose bull, nose up in open field.
No one else could come close to fighting like that.
His clan is roused by powdery dreams
50 And with them all he goes howling
    through sanctuaries.
But would he ever let his child come
To see him ravish others?
"Is this the shepherd of Uruk's flocks,
our strength, our light, our reason,
who hoards the girls of other men
for his own purpose?"
A prayer of opposition rose from Uruk's other men
    to heaven;
and the attentive gods asked:
"Who created this awesome beast
60 with an unmatched strength and a
chant that fosters armies?
This warrior keeps boys from fathers
in the night and in the day.
Is this Gilgamesh,
is this the shepherd of Uruk's flocks,
our strength, our light, our reason,

who hoards the girls of other men
for his own purpose?"
When Anu in the sky heard this,

70   he said to Aruru, great goddess of creation
     that she is:
"You created humans; create again in the
image of Gilgamesh and let this imitation be
as quick in heart and as strong in arm
so that these counterforces might first engage,
then disengage, and finally let Uruk's children
live in peace."
Hearing that, Aruru thought of Anu. Then she
wet her creative fingers, fashioned a rock,
     and tossed
it as far as she could into the woods.

80   Thus she fathered Enkidu, a forester, and gave birth
in terror and in fright without a single cry of pain,
bringing forth another likeness of Ninurta,
     god of war.
Hair covered his body and his curls resembled
those of any good girl, growing swiftly like the
fair hair of Nisaba-giver-of-grain.
This Enkidu had neither clan nor race. He went
clothed as one who shepherds well, eating the food
of grass, drinking from the watery holes of herds
and racing swift as wind or silent water.

90   Then Enkidu met a hunter at the watery hole
on three consecutive days.
And each time the face of the hunter signaled
recognition of Enkidu.
For the herds were uninvited at
the hunter's oasis and the hunter was
disturbed by this intrusion. His quiet heart
rushed up in trouble. His eyes darkened.
Fear leaped forth onto a face that looks
as if it expects to doubt for a long, long time.

His strength is like Anu's swift star, and
tirelessly does he roam across the land...
like the beasts,
(figure 20)

Column iii

100   Then with trembling lips the hunter told his father
      this complaint:
  "Sir, one has come to my watery hole from afar and
  he is the biggest and best throughout the land.
      He feels power.
  His is a strength like that of Anu's swift star, and
  tirelessly does he roam across the land.
  He eats the food of beasts and, like the beasts,
  he comes at will to drink from my watery hole.
  In fear do I see him come to undo
  what I have done by wrecking traps, by
  bursting mounds, by letting animals slip through my
110   grasp, beasts that I would bind."
  Then with hateful lips, the father told the hunter
      his reply:
  "Boy, your answer lies in Uruk where
  there stalks a man of endless strength named
  Gilgamesh.
  He is the biggest and best throughout the land.
      He feels power.
  His is a strength like that of Anu's swift star.
  Start out toward Uruk's ancient palace
  and tell your tale to Gilgamesh.
  In turn he'll say to set a trap, take back with
  you a fine lover, some sacred temple girl,
120   who might let him see what force and charm
      a girl can have.
  Then as Enkidu comes again to the watery hole,
  let her strip in nearby isolation to show him
      all her grace.
  If he is drawn toward her, and leaves the herd
      to mate,
  his beasts on high will leave him then behind."
  The hunter heard his father well and went that very
  night to Uruk where he said this to Gilgamesh

"There is someone from afar whose
force is great throughout our land.
His is a strength throughout the land.
   He feels power.
130   His is a strength like that of Anu's swift star, and
tirelessly does he roam across the land.
He eats the food of beasts and, like the beasts,
he comes at will to drink from my watery hole.
In fear do I see him come to undo
what I have done by wrecking traps, by
bursting mounds, by letting animals slip through my
grasp, beasts that I would bind."
So Gilgamesh replied:
   "Go set a trap; take back with
140   you a fine lover, Shamhat, the sacred temple girl,
who might let him see what charm and force
   a girl can have.
Then as Enkidu comes again to the watery hole,
let her strip in nearby isolation to show him
   all her grace.
If he is drawn toward her, and leaves the herd
   to mate,
his beasts on high will leave him then behind."
The hunter returned, bringing with him
   the sacred temple girl,
and swift was their journey.
Three days later, at the watery hole, they set their
trap for Enkidu and spoke no word for two
150   whole days waiting and waiting and waiting.
Then the herd came slowly in to drink.

Column iv

Beasts arose and sleepy limbs began to flutter then.
Enkidu, the boy who walked on mountains,
who eats the food of beasts and, like the beasts,
comes down at will to drink from the watery hole,
with the beasts arose and stretched

let her strip in nearby isolation to show him all her
grace. If he is drawn toward her and leaves the herd
to mate, his beasts on high will leave him then behind.
(*figure 21*)

his tired limbs to start the day.
She beheld him then, as he was in his beginning,
the one who gave and took life from the far woods.
160 "Here is he, fine lover; be set to wet him with
your tongue and chest and loins.
Spread forth your happiness. Display your
hidden charm.
Jump him fast and kneel upon his shoulders.
Without his wind then, he'll enter near
your entrance.
Take off your robe to let him in.
Let him see what force a girl can have.
The friends he has from on wild will exile him
if he presses his person, as he will, into your
scented bush."
Shamhat let her garments loose and spread forth
170 her happiness which Enkidu entered as
gusts of wind
enter tunnels bound for Hell.
Hot and swollen first, she jumped him fast
knocking out his rapid breath with
thrust after loving thrust.
She let him see what force a girl can have,
and he stayed within her scented bush for
seven nights, leaping, seeping, weeping, and
sleeping there.
After that week of pleasure,
Enkidu returned to the herds
180 but the beasts fled from him in haste.
They stampeded away from his new self.
He could no longer race as he had once,
legs soft now and ankles stiff. The beasts
left him behind and he grew sad
that he could no longer speed with them.
But he enjoyed the memory that no virgin has
and, returning to his fine lover, he once
more knelt between her legs
as she spoke these words to him:

190 "Now you are as if a god, my boy,
with no more need of dumb beasts, however fair.
We can now ascend the road to Uruk's palace,
the immaculate domicile,
    where Anu and Ishtar dwell,
and there we will see Gilgamesh, the powerful,
who rides over the herd like any great king."
These words he heard and he stared at her.
For the first time he wished for just one friend.
Then Enkidu asked the love who was so fine:
"Please come with me and be my love
200 at the immaculate domicile,
    where Anu and Ishtar dwell,
and there we will see Gilgamesh, the powerful,
who rides over the herd like any great king.
I wish to call on him; to proclaim all things
aloud and find a friend in him."

Column v

Enkidu continued:
"Uruk will hear me say, 'I am the strongest.
I alone can do all I wish.'
Forester that I am, a mountainous power is mine.
We should march together, face-by-face,
210 so I can promote your fame."
Then fine lover said these words in invitation:
"Enter Uruk of the herds, Enkidu,
where costumes bright are worn,
where it is always time to party,
where merry music never fades,
where graceful girls do ever play
with toys and boys and men;
for in the night these revelers do
their best to rule the town.
220 There, with a smile, Enkidu
will see his other self, great Gilgamesh.
Watch him all, please. Note his

face, his fists, his fairest sword,
and all the strength that dwells in him.
Could he be greater than you,
this one who's up and down all day and night?
Fear your own anger, boy; for great Gilgamesh
adores fair Shamash and is adored in turn.
Anu of the blue sky, Enlil from the clouds
230 and clever Ea have empowered him.
And before he even sees you,
this great Gilgamesh will have first envisioned you
in Uruk as a rival in a dream."
Gilgamesh awakens to ask his mother, Ninsun,
to leave off the dream.
"Mother," says he, "I saw a star
within my head in sleep just now
that fell at me like Anu's dart
and I could not escape.
240 Uruk was on high of it,
our people did applaud,
and gathered up to praise his force.
Men clenched fists; women danced.
And I too embraced this rising star,
as a man does the woman he loves best,
then took the new one here to you
so that you could see us both at once."
Gilgamesh's mother, who is wise in all
    and worries not, replied:
"This bright, new star is your true friend
250 who fell at you like Anu's dart,
whom you could not escape."

Column vi

Then she who is wise in all
    and worries not continued:
"So say this friend is one who is almighty,
with strength renowned around the world,
like Anu's dart his force is real

She let him see what force a girl can have
(figure 22)

so that he draws you in, as does a spouse,
though he is sure to race away, like
that most distant star, with the secrets
  of your origin.
This dissolves your sleep."
260 Then again, Gilgamesh said to her in reply:
"Mother, I slept when some with axes then
attacked the herds of Uruk."
So Ninsun reassured the frightened king,
"Enkidu will help.
He will guard his loves
or rescue them from danger;
he is your most faithful friend.
Expect him to shepherd you
and to be sure that all goes well."
270 Gilgamesh said to his fond source:
"I pray for fortune and for fate
to send me such a one
that I may have a friend who's as kind
and patient as a brother."
Then in sleep full of repose
the temple girl enchanted Enkidu
where they lay smiling.

Tablet II
Columns i - vi

The Meeting of Gilgamesh and Enkidu

Column i

Then Gilgamesh explained his dream to Ninsun:
   "Last night a vision filled my head
with sights of stars and one sent down from heaven.
At first I tried and failed to carry forth
these signs with me. Then all citizens
of Uruk here assisted in my efforts.
So I was able then to bring these omens
   near to you."
And she said in reply:
"Wisely done, fair son, and rightly so
10 for one well reared as you were.
All others too will soon acclaim
this god-sent gift to you."
Then Gilgamesh concluded:
"In another dream I saw an ax
and bent toward it with manly interest;
so fair was its appearance
that it seemed wholesome, young and
ready as a woman."

Column ii

Soon the day came when the fine lover
   of Enkidu said:
20 "Now come with me to enter into Uruk
where we shall meet the mighty king,
enormous Gilgamesh.
Now you are as if a god, my boy,
with no more need of dumb beasts, however fair.
We can ascend the road to Uruk's palace,
the immaculate domicile, where Anu and Ishtar
   dwell
and there we will see Gilgamesh, the powerful,
who rides over the herd like any great king.
You will see in him a power rare
30 and fairly learn to love him like yourself."

They journeyed from the forest far and wide
to venture on toward Uruk.
The girl led forth the naked boy
as gently as a mother would,
tearing her garment right in two
to hide their native beauty
and clothed his splendid body then
with her own cloak as they approached.

Column iii

Along the way he learned new human ways
40   tracking down the gentle sheep
and using weapons for the first time
to fight away the savage beasts
that do attack the herds and
farms of men.

Column iv

Along the way he also learned to eat and drink
as men and women do. The girl did
teach all these things too for Enkidu's first lessons.
And with a man upon the road they spoke
to learn of customs new to one from
50   far off woods. So Enkidu came then
to know of Gilgamesh who harshly
ruled and was not loved by those men whose girls
he often played with all night long,
And before they entered through the
gates of Uruk's mighty walls, Enkidu
was hailed as one who might
be sent to rival any king who
might treat gentle folk unfairly.

So the mighty brothers fought at first
pushing and shoving each other
for hours and hours enraged.
(figure 23)

Column v

In the alleys of Uruk
60   during a display of force
the approach of Enkidu stopped everything.
Uruk rose before him.
The mountain beyond stretched skyward.
All creatures worshiped him.
Youths rallied round.
People adored him as they adore a newborn babe.
For so it is when one comes from nowhere
to do what no one thought could be done.
For Ishara then a wedding bed is set this night
70   because a guest has come who is as strong
   as any king.
And Enkidu stood before the gate where
   new lovers go
and stopped Gilgamesh from coming with
   nighttime girls.
It is there where they first fight
throughout the night and round about Uruk's walls
which they chipped and wrecked in places.

Column vi

So the mighty brothers fought at first
pushing and shoving each other
for hours and hours enraged.
Then a calm force gently soothed
80   their well-matched spirits
to bring a peace and rest their strife.
It was Enkidu who sued for rest saying:
"Gilgamesh, enough! I am here to
match some fate with you, not
to destroy or rival any king."

Tablet III

Columns i - vi

A Sacred Friendship Forged

The Plot to Conquer Humbaba

TABLET III

Column i

Then Enkidu and Gilgamesh joined in sacred
friendship and sealed their solemn
bond with noble kiss.

Column ii

Enkidu and Gilgamesh often sat then together,
visited Ninsun's shrine, conversed
of many plans and fashioned a future together.
Once, informed by fears of
future sorrow, Enkidu began
to weep and warn his friend of
10   coming horror. He said:
"If we go there beyond here to where
Humbaba-the-awful lives,
there will be a gruesome war
in a place no one calls home,
where no one wants to stay for long
or go to rest or rest to gain
the strength to reach the forests."
The Great One rose within
and robed herself appropriately
20   covering herself,
ringing her curls beneath her crown
to ascend the altar, where she stood
lighting the first signals of charcoal
  for the incense
and preparing sacred cups that hold the
precious liquids which will be spilled.
Then Ninsun asked Shamash:
"Why?
Why have you called my only son away
and shaped his mind in so disturbed a way?
30   For now, he says, you invite him to begin a

pilgrimage that ends where Humbaba
directs a never ending battle,
along a foreign, lonely road
far within the forests dark and damp
where a man like him might just kill
a god like Humbaba or be killed
to dissolve the pain that you, Shamash, oppose."

Column iii

Humbaba stirs within the darkened wood
and in the hearts of men there rises fear.
40   When Enkidu spoke at last to Gilgamesh
he said these words of warning:
"I knew this monster's reputation long ago.
Fire and death mix in his breath,
and I for one do not wish now
to challenge such a demon."
But Gilgamesh retorted: "All glory
will be ours if now we conquer
this unprecedented foe and risk the
woe that frightens others."
50   And Enkidu said then in swift reply:
"How shall we go towards woods
so fiercely guarded?"

Column iv

Enlil it was who sent Humbaba there
to scare away intruders with fierce
and frightening howls. Great Gilgamesh
remembered that when he spoke words like these
to Enkidu: "Only gods live forever
with Shamash, my friend; for even our
longest days are numbered. Why worry over
60   being like dust in the wind? Leap up for

this great threat. Fear not. Even if I were
to fail and fall in combat,
all future clans would say I did the job."
Special weapons then were ordered to be made
for their assault upon Humbaba.
Axes, swords, and combat saddles were prepared
and all of Uruk's population flocked round
their great departure.

Column v

The awful monster's reputation
70 made Uruk's gentle people fear
for their great king. And after
all the plans were made to start
out to fight Humbaba, a group
came forward to see the king.
The elders spoke to Gilgamesh:
"Fear the force that you control, hot-headed boy;
Be sure you watch where you direct
your every, heavy swing in battle.
Vanguards protect.
80 Friends save friends.
Let Enkidu lead on the way
through forests that he knows.
He knows how to fight in woodlands;
he knows where to pick his fight.
Enkidu will shield his bosom too
as well as that of his companion
so as to protect them both.
He'll traverse any ditch of any width.
Enkidu will guard our king.
90 Be sure to bring him safely back."
Gilgamesh said to Enkidu:
"Arise, my other self, and speed your way
  to Egalmah
to where my mother sits, kind Ninsun.

She understands all I need to know.
She'll tell us where we should go and what to do."
Again the men embraced as teammates do.
Gilgamesh and Enkidu set out to Egalmah.

Column vi

Upset by all his thoughts of coming battles
and concerned by his consultations with the gods,
100 Gilgamesh then sadly set his palace rooms in order.
His weapons were prepared, his helmet shined
and garments freshly cleaned.
Citizens of Uruk came to say good-bye and
wish their daring king farewell.
"Go careful through this risky, bold adventure,
mighty lord. Be sure of your own safety first of all."
So spoke the elders of his town and then continued:
"Let Enkidu take risks for you and have him
lead the way through woods he knows so well.
110 Pray that Shamash show him, as your guide,
the nearest path and choicest route to
where you dare to go.
May great Lugalbanda favor you in combat
  with Humbaba."
Then Enkidu himself spoke finally to his king:
"The time is right for us to now depart.
Follow me, sir, along the savage way
to where a worthy opponent,
the awful beast Humbaba,
waits for your challenge in the
120 dark woodlands that he guards.
Do not fear this. Rely on me
in every matter and let me act
as careful guide for your most daring venture."

THE EPIC OF GILGAMESH

Tablet IV

Columns i - vi

A Mother's Prayer

Journey to the Cedar Forest

An Ominous Wound

Columns i, ii

Ten miles into the march, they stopped to eat.
  After thirty miles, they rested,
then finished another twenty miles that day.
Within three days they covered
what would take others a month and a half to travel.
They dug for water where
there appeared to be none
in the dry desert on their way
to challenge Humbaba.

Columns iii, iv

10 Onward ventured Gilgamesh and Enkidu
And they both knew where danger lurked
at their first destination.
As up they climbed upon the final hill,
they saw a guard put out by Humbaba
as fierce as any watchdog.
Gilgamesh pursued first.

Column v

Gilgamesh heard shouts from
Enkidu who said to his companion:
"Remember promises we made
20 in the city where we live. Recall
the courage and the force
we vowed to bring upon this mission."
These words dispelled the fear felt
in his heart and Gilgamesh in
return then shouted back:
"Quick. Grab the guard
and don't let go.

Humbaba stirs within the darkened wood
and in the hearts of men there rises fear.
...
Fire and death mix in his breath.
(*figure 24*)

Race fearlessly and don't let go.
Our enemy, Humbaba, has set out seven uniforms
30   but has only dressed in one
so far. So six layers of strength
are yet unused by him."
As one mad brute he is enraged,
bellowing loudly while the foresters warn each
    other
what he's like.

Column vi

Wounded in combat with the guard they killed,
Enkidu uses words to say:
"I lost my strength in this crushed hand
    when the gate slammed shut.
What shall I do?"
40   Then Gilgamesh spoke: "Brother,
as a man in tears would,
you transcend all the rest who've gathered,
for you can cry and kill
with equal force.
Hold my hand in yours,
and we will not fear what hands like ours can do.
Scream in unison, we will ascend
to death or love, to say in song what we shall do.
Our cry will shoot afar so
50   this new weakness, awful doubt,
will pass through you.
Stay, brother, let us ascend as one."

THE EPIC OF GILGAMESH

Tablet V

Columns i, iii, iv, vi

A Dream of Battle

Humbaba Slain

Column i

Gilgamesh and Enkidu froze and stared
        into the woods'
great depth and height. When they spied
Humbaba's path, they found the opening toward
straight passage. Then they were able to find
    and see
the home of the gods, the paradise of Ishtar's
    other self,
called Irnini-most-attractive.
All beauty true is ever there
where gods do dwell, where there is
cool shade and harmony and
10   sweet-odored food to match their mood.

Column iii

Then Gilgamesh envisioned yet again
another dream
high up in the hills
where boulders crashed.
Again Enkidu said to his brother,
as he unraveled this dreary story for his king:
"Brother, your song is a fine omen.
This dream will make you well.
Brother, that vision you saw is rich
20   for on that mountain top
we can capture Humbaba and
hurl his earthly form from
towering cliffs through sky to
earth, making his shape
as flat and wide as it is round and high."
"Mountain, mountain in the sky,
Break the god and make him die."

Column iv

Mountain-on-high then sent the myth
  into Enkidu's sleep,
and a chill from the high winds forced him to rest,
30 since he was blown around as grain is
  on an open field.
Curled up in a ball, Gilgamesh rested
in blessed sleep, the best of friends
  at the worst of times.
But by the moon's half way course, he rose
and then began to speak:
"Brother, if you made no noise, what sound
  woke me?
If you didn't jostle me, what shook my body?
There was no god nearby, so why am I so stunned?
Brother, I've had a third vision in sleep
and I am deeply frightened to recall it all.
40 Sky screamed. And Mother Earth moaned.
Sun went out of light and blackest night
enveloped the heavens.
Then came flashes of lightning, source of fire.
Storm clouds raced nearby and swept all life away
from out of the sky above our heads.
Brightness dissolved, light evaporated;
cinders turned to ash.
When we leave the mountain, this is
  what we will remember."
When Enkidu learned this myth as told,
50 he replied to Gilgamesh:
"Shamash, your god, creates a great attraction
for both of us. Shamash now approves
of this attack upon Humbaba. Take the sign
as some divine dream to urge us on."
Shamash himself said such words to Gilgamesh
as if in prayer:
"Do not balk now, favored one.
Brace yourself for battle and proceed."

Heavenly winds blasted down from out of the sky
60   about and all around Humbaba. From east and
west, with sand and grain, they blew him
back and forth. His giant self became
fatigued. His awesome strength dwindled.
Not even his great right foot could step away
    in flight.
So in this way, by Shamash's intervention,
Humbaba-the-awful beast was brought so low.

Column vi

The dying beast called out for mercy once
and part of what he said could still be heard
    over the howling winds:
"Please, Gilgamesh! Have mercy on me, wounded.
70   I shall freely give you all the lumber
    of my mighty realm
and work for you both day and night."
It was Enkidu then who shouted louder
than the beast and with his words he
urged a swift conclusion:
"Kill the beast now, Gilgamesh. Show
no weak or silly mercy toward so sly a foe."
Taking his companion's mean advice, Gilgamesh
swiftly cut the beast, splattering blood upon
his cloak and sandals then. Soiled by this
80   violent conflict, the friends began their
journey back to Uruk's towering walls
expecting now to be received as heroes who
had fought and won a legendary battle.

THE EPIC OF GILGAMESH
Tablet VI

Ishtar's Proposal

A Scathing Rejection

Ishtar's Revenge: The Bull of Heaven

The Slaughter of the Bull

Enkidu's Ominous Dream

G ilgamesh bathed himself and cleaned his hair,
   as beautiful as it was long.
He cast off bloodied robes and put on
    his favorite gown,
secured the cincture and stood royal.
Then Gilgamesh put on his crown.
Ishtar looked up at Gilgamesh's handsome pride.
"Come to me," she whispered. "Come to me and be
    my groom.
Let me taste all parts of you,
treat you as husband, be treated as your wife.

10 And as a gift I'd give to you
one regal coach of gold and blue
with wheels of yellow and all so new
that I would flatter all your might
with the sight of demons driven off
by my own god, by my own man.
Come to my home, most sweetly scented
    of all places,
where holy faces wash your feet with tears as
do the priests and priestesses of gods like Anu.
All mighty hands of kings and queens

20 will open doors for you.
So too will all the countryside donate
in duplicate to your fold.
And the slow will race ahead for you,
so that by association, all that you touch
will turn to gold."
Gilgamesh replied to mighty Ishtar thus:
"But how could I repay you as a wife
and still avoid the bitterness and strife
    that follow you?
Is it perfume for a dress you want, or me?

30 My self or something wrapped around a tree?
Do I offer you food, sweet nuts or grapes?
Are those for gods or for the savage apes?
And who will pour a treat to us in bed,
you dressed for life and me as if I'm dead?

Here's a song I made for you
(a little crude, a little rude):
Ishtar's the hearth gone cold,
a broken door, without the gold;
a fort that shuts its soldiers out,
40   a water well that's filled with doubt;
tar that can't be washed away,
a broken cup, stained and gray;
rock that shatters to dust and sand,
a useless weapon in the hand;
and worse than that or even this,
a god's own sandal filled with piss.
You've had your share of boys, that's true,
but which of them came twice for you?
Let me now list the ones that you just blew away.
50   First was Tammuz, the virgin boy you took
after a three-year-long seductive look.
Then you lusted for a fancy, colored bird
and cut its wing so it could not herd.
Thus in the lovely woods at night
bird sings, 'I'm blind. I have no sight.'
You trapped a lion, too, back then.
Its cock went in your form-as-hen.
And then you dug him seven holes
in which to fall on sharpened poles.
60   You let a horse in your back door
by laying on a stable floor;
but then you built the world's first chain
to choke his throat and end his reign.
You let him run with all his might,
as boys will sometimes do at night,
before you harnessed his brute force
with labor fierce, a mean divorce.
So did his mother weep and wail
to see her child's foot set with a nail.
70   You fondled once a shepherd boy
who baked buns for your tongue's joy
and daily killed his lambs so coy.

...Loose the bull who could trample him at once.
Let the bull spill his blood.
(figure 25)

So in return for gifts like those
you chose to lupinize his toy.
And when his brothers saw his penis
they knew you'd done something heinous.
Ishullanu trimmed your father's trees
and brought you carrots, dates and peas.
So mighty you sat down to feasts,
80   then turned your thoughts to raping beasts.
You saw him naked once and said:
'Come, Ishullanu, into my bed
and force your force into my head.
Place your fingers where men dread
to touch a girl who's dead.'
And he in turn said this to you:
'What is it that you'd have me do?
I know, kind mother, I won't eat
if I can't match your female heat.
90   But would you have me sing and sin
as my whistle goes both out and in?'
So since he balked to play that role,
you switched his jewel into a mole;
stuck in the muck of a marshy town
his pleasure can't go up or down.
And that is how you'd deal with me
if we got friendly, warm, and free."
When Ishtar heard his words so cruel,
she lost her cool and played the fool
100   by blasting off for daddy's distant star,
where she said: "Daddy, daddy, daddy, please,
Gilgamesh called me a tease."
"Gilgamesh said I sinned and lived
without faith in myself or others," she pouted.
Her father, Anu, said these exact words to Ishtar:
"Now, daughter, did you first insult him,
this Gilgamesh who then began to taunt you
with jibes about your inclinations?"
Ishtar shouted back at him-who-is-her-father:
"You! Now! Make him stop! Loose the

bull who could trample him at once.
Let the bull spill his blood.
And you'd better do this now or I'll
wreak havoc of my own right down to Hell.
I'll loose the goddamn devil. I'll rain corpses.
I'll make zombies eat infants and there will be
more dead souls than living ones!"
Her father, Anu, said these exact words to Ishtar:
"But if I do what you seem now to want,
120   there would be long years of drought
and sorrow. Have you stored enough
reserve to feed the people who
deserve your close protection?"
And she said:
"Yes, I have reserved a plan
for those I love. Now do as I demand
and punish all who insult me."
Then her father, Anu, heard Ishtar's cry
and Ishtar forced her will.
130   Anu set loose a bull from out of the sky and,
at the bull's proclamation, there cracks the
earth to swallow up nine dozen citizens of Uruk!
An earthquake fixed a grave for nine dozen
   citizens of Uruk.
Two or three or four hundred victims,
maybe more than that, fell into Hell.
And when the quake returned for a third time,
it was near to Enkidu,
he who fell upon the Abyss so wide and grim.
Enkidu collapsed near the earth-shaking bull.
140   Then he leaped to grab the bull by his long horns
even with spit upon his face from out
   the savage mouth,
even with the stench of bowels near his nose.
Then Enkidu said to Gilgamesh:
"Brother, you and I are now hailed as one.
How could we defeat a god?
Brother, I see great challenge here, but can we dare

defy such force?
Let's kill it if we can right now.
Be unrelenting and hope that god
gives us the strength.
150 We must be cold and strong
to cut our enemy's weak neck."
Enkidu surrounds the bull, pursuing Heaven's beast
and finally catches him.
So Gilgamesh, like a bull dancer,
svelte and mighty then,
plunged his sword into the throat held fast
by Enkidu.
They butchered and bled the bull and then cut out
its heart
to offer as sacrifice before Shamash.
Then Gilgamesh and Enkidu retreated
160 from the altar itself and stood afar
in deep respect as they did pray.
At last the two sat down, bound by war,
bound by worship.
Ishtar appeared upon Uruk's walls
looking like a wailing widow.
She shrieked this curse aloud:
"Damn Gilgamesh, who injured me,
by slaughtering a divine bull."
Enkidu reacted to these words of Ishtar quick
by hurling at her head a hunk of meat
from the bull's thigh.
170 And from afar he shouted up to her:
"This bloody mess of a plain bull would
be about what I could make of you
if you came near. I'd tie
your hands with these rope-like intestines."
Ishtar signaled then for her attendants:
coiffured bishops, cantors, and girls
whose charms keep worshippers coming.
Then atop the great wall above the city high
standing by the severed part of its right thigh,

180 she had them shriek laments for the bull
      who'd died.
    So to complete this ritual and adorn his throne
    Gilgamesh summoned artisans of all kinds.
    Some measured the diameter of the bull's horns,
    each containing thirty pounds of lapis lazuli.
    Together those horns could hollow hold
    half a dozen quarts of oil.
    And that is what Gilgamesh brought as potion
    to the altar of Lugalbanda, his special protector.
    He carried the horns and enshrined them
      in a palace
190 of honor where his clan held rites.
    Then Enkidu and Gilgamesh absolved their
    bloody hands in the forgiving river,
    the deep, eternal Euphrates that does not change.
    At last relieved of such a stain, the friends renew
    their vows with a brief embrace
    before riding through Uruk's crowded streets
    amid acclaim. There Gilgamesh stops to
    give this speech to gathered girls:
    "What man is most impressive now?
200 Who is finest, firmest, and most fair?
    Isn't Gilgamesh that man above men
    and isn't Enkidu the strongest of all?"
    Then they party loudly throughout the day
    so that, come night, they drop down dead in sleep.
    But Enkidu is resurrected quickly
    to relieve his soul of fright
    and sadly he asks Gilgamesh in tears:
    "Oh brother, why would I dream that gods sat round
      to set my fate?"

Tablet VII
Columns i, iii, iv

The Death of Enkidu

Column i

Enkidu confessed this dream to Gilgamesh:
"The gods all gathered round last night
and Anu told Enlil that one of us should die
because of what we've done against their names.
Though Shamash intervened for us,
saying we had slain Humbaba and the bull
with his consent, the others sought revenge."
Then Enkidu fell ill and soon lost his full strength.
Saying words like these as his friend lay dying,
10   Gilgamesh intoned:
"Why should you be so condemned and why should
I go right on living?
Will my own sad eyes soon never look on you again?
Shall I descend to depths beneath
this earth to visit worlds reserved
for those who've died?"
Enkidu glanced up, addressing the entryway
on which his hand was morbidly crushed:
"Door of all forests, that confuses wind and rain,
20   deaf, dumb, and blind portal;
I admired your firm texture
before I first saw the mighty trees
aloft that gave force to you.
There is nothing on earth that could replace
your splendor or your worth.
At two hundred feet in height, at forty feet
  around are
your mighty posts, your priceless hinge
cut and crafted in Nippur's holy ground.
If I had guessed that you'd become this,
30   I would have shattered you to pieces
with my ax and have been more careful not
to wound my hand so badly on your frame."

Column iii

Then cursing the hunter whom he first met
and the girl whom he first loved, Enkidu raged:
"Slash him. Cut half his face.
Raise up floods beneath his feet
so that no animal is safe."
And at his sacred, former lover Enkidu did swear:
"Get up, witch, and hear your fortune
40   guaranteed now and forever.
I damn you off and damn you down.
I'd break your teeth with stones and let
your mouth hang open
until you'd say thanks to your killer
who would favor you by letting you
lie homeless on an open road
in some foul ditch.
May all and any who can hurt you now
often cross the paths you take. I
50   hope you live in fright, unsure of hope
and starved always for the touch of love."
Shamash responded from on high:
"The fine lover, my Enkidu, is cursed by you
who gave you bread and meat and stew,
the same who offered you some wine,
food and drink almost divine
so that you were taken for a god.
The fine lover, my thoughtless boy, invested you
with robes of gold, robes of blue
60   and, more important, gave your dear friend
the thought that he should do whatever need
be done and still more too.
Did your brother, Gilgamesh, give you as fine a bed
as any on earth or any there in heaven?
Did he promote the likes of you to fame
unrivaled, so that rulers kneel to kiss
the ground you walk upon?

He will also show the Uruk people how
   to mourn for you.
An entire people will cry upon your death
70   and he will go in tears
ignoring the dirt and dust and mud
that stain his hands and hair.
So in despair will his mind be
as off he roams in lonely woods wearing rags."
When Enkidu heard these sad words
he was speechless and in his heart
he knew that Shamash spoke the truth.
His anger fled and Enkidu resolved
to die in peace.

Column iv

80   With these last words the dying Enkidu did pray
and say to his beloved companion:
"In dreams last night
the heavens and the earth poured out
great groans while I alone
stood facing devastation. Some fierce
and threatening creature flew down at me
and pushed me with its talons toward
the horror-filled house of death
wherein Irkalla, queen of shades,
90   stands in command.
There is darkness which lets no person
again see light of day.
There is a road leading away from
bright and lively life.
There dwell those who eat dry dust
and have no cooling water to quench
   their awful thirst.
As I stood there I saw all those who've died
and even kings among those darkened souls
have none of their remote and former glory.

100   All earthly greatness was forfeit
and I entered then into the house of death.
Others who have been there long
did rise to welcome me."
Hearing this, great Gilgamesh said
  to his handsome mother:
"My friend, dear Enkidu, has seen his passing now
and he lies dying here upon a sad and lonely cot.
Each day he weakens more and wonders
  how much more
life may yet belong to his hands
  and eyes and tongue."
Then Enkidu resumed his last remarks and said:
110 "Oh Gilgamesh, some destiny has robbed me
of the honor fixed for those who die in battle.
I lie now in slow disgrace, withering day by day,
deprived as I am of the peace that comes to one
who dies suddenly in a swift clash of arms."

Tablet VIII

Columns i - iii, v

Gilgamesh's Lament

The Specter of Mortality

Farewell to Enkidu

TABLET VIII

Column i

Then once again at break of day
did Gilgamesh conclude the silent night
by being first to raise his hands and voice
and he said:
"Oh Enkidu, whose own mother's grace
was every bit as sweet as any deer's
and whose father
raced just as swift and stood as strong
as any horse that ever ran,
10   accept all natural customs
within the limitless confines of the wild
where you were raised by those with
tails, by those with hooves, by
those with fur and whiskers.
All the roads in and out of your great forest
now lie silent, but for the sobbing done
  by your wild friends.
The aged men and women of Uruk mourn today
and raise their withered palms in prayer
as we carry you by, toward Mount Kur.
20   Grottos weep for you and valleys too
and so do those great trees
upon the shore where you loved to run.
And also crying now are
large bears, little dogs, baby cubs
of lions and of tigers, and even
the hyena now has ceased its laugh.
Wild bull and the rapidest of deer
All, all, all sigh,
All, all, all cry for you.
30   Ulay's lovely riverbanks are swollen on this day
where you did walk as boys alone can do
upon the banks of rivers that mother
their young thoughts about life and death.

My friend has died and half my heart is torn from me
Won't I soon be like him, stone cold and dead for all
the days to come?
(*figure 26*)

Yes, that great brown god, the river Ulay,
today mourns for you as does the
true Euphrates eternal and silent.
Uruk's rugged men mourn for you
who killed that sacrificial bull.
They all weep tears today
40   and those in Eridu, who loved your fame,
and say your name aloud,
they too weep tears today
and all in days to come, even those who knew
you not, all may weep tears someday
for your sad lot.
Your favorite aunt, your blessed servant,
your first girlfriend,
your inspiration, your companion, your darling
dear and she you feared to be alone with,
50   all women who ever sat and ate with you,
all men you ever helped with food or drink,
every one and all,
lovers fast and strangers slow.
Those you touched or who touched you
and those who never knew just how you felt.
All and every burst into tears
today because they heard that
you were suddenly dead."

Column ii

"I'll cry now, citizens of Uruk, and you
60   will finally hear what no one else
has ever had the nerve to say in sorrow.
I was family and friend to Enkidu and I shall
fill the woodlands where we stalked
   with loud, sad sobs today.
I cry now, Enkidu, like some crazed woman.
   I howl.
I screech for you because you were the ax
   upon my belt

and the bow in my weak hand; the sword
  within my sheath,
the shield that covered me in battle;
  my happiest robe,
the finest clothes I ever wore,
the ones that made me look best
  in the eyes of the world.
70 That is what you were; that is what you'll always be.
What devil came to take you off from me?
Brother, you chased down the strongest mule,
the swiftest horse on mountains high,
the quickest panthers in the flatlands.
And they in turn will weep for you.
Birds in the air cry aloud.
Fish in the lake gather together near the shore.
What else heeds this sorrow?
The leaves of the trees and the paths you loved
80 in the forest grow dark.
Night itself murmurs and so too does the day.
All the eyes of the city that once saw your kind face
  begin to weep.
Why? Because you were my brother and you died.
When we met and fought and loved,
we went up on mountains high to where we dared
  to capture
god's own strength in one great beast and then
  to cut its throat,
thus humbling Humbaba, green god
  of woodlands steep.
Now there is a sleep-like spell on you, and you
are dark as well as deaf."
90 Enkidu can move no more.
Enkidu can lift his head no more.
"Now there is a sound throughout the land
that can mean only one thing.
I hear the voice of grief and I know
  that you have been taken
somewhere by death.

Weep. Let the roads we walked together
  flood themselves with tears.
Let the beasts we hunted cry out for this:
the lion and the leopard, the tiger and the panther.
Let their strength be put into their tears.
100 Let the cloud-like mountain where you killed
the guardian of woodland treasures
place grief upon its sky-blue top.
Let the river which soothed our feet overflow
  its banks
as tears do that swell and rush across
  my dusty cheeks.
Let the clouds and stars race swiftly with you
  into death.
Let the rain that makes us dream
tell the story of your life tonight.
Who mourns for you now, Brother?
Everyone who knew you does.
110 The harvesters and the farmers
  who used to bring you grain
are standing alone in their fields.
The servants who worked in your house
today whispered your name in empty rooms.
The lover who kissed every part of you
touches her chilled lips with scented fingers.
The women of the palace sit
and stare at the queen of the city.
She sobs and sobs and sobs.
The men with whom you played so bold
120 speak fondly of your name.
Thus they deal with this misfortune.
But what do I do? I only know that a cruel fate
  robbed me
of my dearest friend too soon.
What state of being holds you now? Are you
  lost forever?
Do you hear my song?"

"I placed my hand upon your quiet heart."
One brother covered the set face of another
with a bride-white veil.
"I flew above you then as if I were an eagle."
130 Then, like some great cat whose darling young
    have sadly died,
    Gilgamesh slides back and forth fixed mindlessly
    on grief.
    He commands many men to erect statues of honor,
    saying:
    "Make his chest a noble blue
    and on his honored body place a jewel
    as will allow all viewers then to see
    how great he was,
    how great he'll always be."
    Next day, Gilgamesh rose from a restless sleep.

Column iii

Then Gilgamesh continued with his bird-like words:
"On a pedestal I will honor your corpse
by setting you
140 above all earthly princes who will celebrate you
    when people from all distant lands
    both rich and poor in spirit
    acclaim your memory.
    And when you are gone,
    never again to wear good clothes or care for food,
    I'll still remember how you dressed
      and how you ate."
    When day did break again next morn,
    Gilgamesh stripped off the lion's cloak and
    rose to say this prayer:
150 "Your funeral is a precious
    gesture I made to hide my own guilt."
    Goodbye, dear brother
    Ave atque vale, frater (1)
    Sat sri akai meri pra (2)

TABLET VIII

Dehna hune wood wordema (3)
Slan agat, seanchara (4)
Shalom.(5)

Column v

Still grieving reverently
after he arose next day, Gilgamesh imagined
  the Annunaki
160 who decide the fate of
those who go to the underworld.
After learning how to pause his heart,
Gilgamesh created just the same image
in the face of a river.
At break of day,
on the sacred table made of special wood,
the grieving king placed a consecrated bowl of blue
filled with butter and with honey too
and this he offered up in solemn prayer
170 to Shamash, lord god.

1. Latin: Hail and farewell, Brother
2. Bengali (India): Goodbye, Brother
3. Amharic (Ethiopia): Farewell, sweet Brother
4. Gaelic: Go fairly, old friend
5. Hebrew: Peace

so like a savage beast just then
did he bring death again and again
upon the lions' heads
(*figure 27*)

Column i

Then Gilgamesh wept some more for his dead
friend. He wandered
over barren hills, mumbling to his own spirit:
"Will you too die as Enkidu did?
Will grief become your food? Will we both
fear the lonely hills, so vacant?
I now race from place to place,
dissatisfied with wherever I am and
turn my step toward Utnapishtim,
10   godchild of Ubaratutu,
who lives a pious life in fair Dilmun
where the morning sun arises as it
does in paradises lost and won.
As if in sleep I come upon the mountain door
  at midnight
where I face wild-eyed lions and I am afraid.
Then to Sin, the god of mighty light,
I raise my solemn chant to beg:
'Save me, please, my god.'"
Despite respite
20   he could not sleep or dream that night.
Instead he wandered through the woods
so like a savage beast just then
did he bring death again and again
upon the lions' heads
with an ax he drew
from off his belt.

Column ii

When he finally reached the base of
Mt. Mashu, Gilgamesh began to
climb the double cliff
30   that guides the rising and setting of Shamash.
Now these identical towers touch

the distant, distant sky,
and far below, their breasts descend toward Hell.
Those who guard the gate are
poison scorpions
who terrorize all, whose spells bring death.
And then resplendent power
thrives all across the town
where I was born
40   and rises farther still to
mountain tops.
At dawn and dark they shield Shamash.
And when he sensed them there,
Gilgamesh could not dare to look
upon their threat;
but held his glance away,
suspended fear,
and then approached in dread.
One among the guardians there
50   said this to his wife:
"The one who comes toward us
is partly divine, my dear."
And then the same one said
to the god-like part of Gilgamesh,
"Eternal heart, why make
this long, long trip
trying to come to us
through travail? Speak now."

Column iii

Gilgamesh said: "I come by here
60   to visit my elder, my Utnapishtim,
the epitome of both life everlasting and
death that is eternal."
The poison scorpion guardian said:
"No mortal man has ever
come to know what you seek
here. Not one of all your kind

has come so far, the distance
you would fall if you fell
all day and all night into the pit
70 and through great darkness
where there is no light
without Shamash who raises
and lowers the sun;
to where I let no one go,
to where I forbid anyone to enter."

Column iv

Heartachest pain abounds
with ice or fire all around.
The scorpion one,
I do not know whether a man or a woman,
80 said then:
"Gilgamesh, I command you
to proceed
to highest peaks
over hills toward heaven.
Godspeed!
With all permissions given here,
    I approve your venture."
So Gilgamesh set out then over
that sacred, sacred path
    within the mountains of Mashu,
near that incarnate ray of sunshine
90 precious to Shamash.
Oh dark, dark, dark, dark.
Oh the night, unholy and blind,
that wrapped him as soon as he stepped
forth upon that path.

So Gilgamesh set out then over
that sacred, sacred path
within the mountains of Mashu,
near that incarnate ray of sunshine
precious to Shamash.
(figure 28)

Column v

DARKNESS
Beneath a moonless, starless sky,
Gilgamesh was frozen and unseeing
by time before midnight;
by midnight's hollow eye
100   he was unseen and frozen.
At 1 a.m. he tripped and fell
blinded and frozen.
At 2 a.m. he staggered on
blinded and frozen.
At 3 a.m. he faltered not
blinded and frozen.
By 4 a.m. his second wind warmed him
    who still was
blinded and frozen.
And at your final dawn,
110   son of man, you will see only
a heap of broken images in an ascending
light that gives you sight you may not want,
for you will then behold all precious goods
and gardens sweet as home to you, as exile,
boughs of blue, oh unforgotten gem,
as true as any other memory from any other
    previous life.

Column vi

Then along the path
Gilgamesh traveled fast
and came at length to
120   shorelines fresh with dew.
And there he met a maiden,
one who knows the secrets of the sea.

THE EPIC OF GILGAMESH
Tablet X
Columns i - vi

Siduri Whose Drinks Refresh the Soul

The Boatman, Urshanabi

Gilgamesh Implores Utnapishtim

Column i

This gentle girl is called Siduri
  and she sits by the sea
where she sways from side to side.
She made the water pale; she crafted
  the first gold bowl
while peeking at the sun
through a slit across her face veil.
King Gilgamesh approached the girl's small cottage
  by the sea
dressed as a mountain man,
a meat-eater,
10 with an aching heart
and the stare of one setting out upon some
arduous, horrid trek.
The girl who gives her men lifesaving drinks
said to herself, "Beware of the one
coming now. He walks as if he'd kill."
And so Siduri locked the door,
put stones in place, lay on the floor.
When Gilgamesh heard sounds inside
he yelled at her. "Why do you hide?
20 Shall I have to break through this door?"
The girl whose drinks refresh the soul
then said these words to Gilgamesh:
"Is there a simple reason, sir, why you're so sad
or why your face is drawn and thin?
Has chance worn out your youth or did some
wicked sorrow consume you like food?
You look like one setting out on some arduous,
  horrid trek,
like one exposed to extremes of hot and cold,
like one who searches everywhere for grace."
30 He responded then to her who gives her men
lifesaving drinks:
"Girl, there is no simple reason why I'm so sad

or why my face is drawn and thin.
Chance alone did not wear out my youth. Some
wicked sorrow consumes me like food.
But I do look like one setting out on some
arduous, horrid trek, like one exposed
to extreme hot or cold,
like one who searches everywhere
40   for the breath of life
because my brother, my only true friend, met death;
he who raced wild horses there,
who caught orange tigers here.
This was Enkidu, my soul's good half,
who raced wild horses there,
who caught orange tigers here;
who did all things while he conquered mountains
and divine bulls that race
across the sky like clouds;
50   who gave Humbaba, the woodland god,
reason to weep when he stole through
the wooded path to slaughter lions."

Column ii

Gilgamesh continued:
"I greatly loved my friend who was always
    there for me.
I loved Enkidu who was always there for me.
What awaits us all caught him first
and I did thirst for one whole week to
see him once again in splendor until
    his body decomposed.
Then I wept for my future death
60   and I fled home for mountaintops to breathe
when my friend's death choked off my wind.
On mountaintops I roamed content to breathe
again when my friend's death choked off my wind.
Walking. Walking. Walking over hills.

Could I sit down to rest?
Could I stop crying then
when my best friend had died
as I will someday do?"
Then Gilgamesh said to the fair girl
70 whose saving drinks gave life to men:
"Tell me, girl, how to get to Utnapishtim.
Where do I look for signs? Show me directions.
  Help.
Please let me have safe passage over seas.
Give me advice to guide me on my way."
She said to him in swift reply:
"No man has ever gone that way
and lived to say he crossed the sea.
Shamash only ventures there,
only Shamash would dare
80 to stare into the sun.
Pain joins the voyager soon,
and soon the traveler grows weary
where death surrounds the path
on every side with danger."

Column iii

The girl whose drinks refresh the soul
then said these words to Gilgamesh:
"Remember always, mighty king,
that gods decreed the fates of all
many years ago. They alone are let
90 to be eternal, while we frail humans die
as you yourself must someday do.
What is best for us to do
is now to sing and dance.
Relish warm food and cool drinks.
Cherish children to whom your love gives life.
Bathe easily in sweet, refreshing waters.
Play joyfully with your chosen wife.

Remember always, mighty king,
that gods decreed the fate of all
many years ago. They alone are let
to be eternal, while we frail humans die
as you yourself must someday do.
What is best for us to do
is now to sing and dance.
Relish warm food and cool drinks.
(figure 29)

It is the will of the gods for you to smile
on simple pleasure in the leisure time
   of your short days.
100 And what, after all, my fellow man,
would you do when you got to that
far side where Urshanabi dwells
among the hills of Utnapishtim?
He knows only the dead weight of what is dead
and he is one who plays with deadly snakes.
Would you put your lips near his?
If he befriends you then, go on.
But if he walks away, return to me."
With that in mind
110 Gilgamesh took up his chore,
unsheathed his sword, slipped toward the shore
and there joined one who rows the seas of death.
Gilgamesh sliced through the underbrush
   as an arrow goes through air
while cracking the stones of the sacred columns.
And Urshanabi barely saw the arrow's glint
and too late heard the ax's thud.
And so surprised was he that
there was never any chance to
hide or to deny the daring man
120 at least a chance at
some safe passage.
Gilgamesh traveled on to where he next
found the ferryman of Utnapishtim. This man,
Urshanabi, said to Gilgamesh:
"Your face seems tense; your eyes
   do not glance well
and Hell itself is part of how you look.
Grief hangs from your shoulders.
You look like one who's been without a home,
   without a bed
or roof for a long time, wandering the wilds
   on some random search."
130 Gilgamesh replied to the ferryman:

"Yes sir, it's true my face is tense
and that my eyes seem harsh.
My looks are now so hellish,
for I wear my grief as ill as any other.
I'm not this way as some refugee
without a bed or roof for a long time,
and I don't wander the wilds randomly.
I grieve for Enkidu, my fair companion
    and true friend,
who chased the strongest mule, the swiftest horse
140 on mountain high, the quickest panther
    of the flatland.
Together we did all things, climbing sky-high peaks,
stealing divine cattle, humbling the gods,
    killing Humbaba
and the precious lions, guardians of the sky.
All this I did with my best friend who now is dead.
Mortality reached him first and I am left this week
to weep and wail for his shriveling corpse
    which scares me.
I roam aloft and alone now, by death enthralled,
and think of nothing but my dear friend.
I roam the lonely path with death upon my mind
150 and think of nothing but my dear friend.
Over many seas and across many mountains I roam.
I can't stop pacing. I can't stop crying.
My friend has died and half my heart
    is torn from me.
Won't I soon be like him, stone-cold and dead,
    for all the days to come?"
Urshanabi replied as he had done before:
"Your face seems tense; your eyes
    do not glance well
and Hell itself is part of how you look.
Grief hangs from your shoulders.
You look like one who's been without a home,
    without a bed

160 or roof for a long time, wandering the wilds
        on some random search."
    And Gilgamesh said to him then in swift reply:
    "Of course my face seems tense
        and my eyes seem harsh.
    Of course I'm worn out weeping. Why should
        I not cry?
    I've come to ask directions to Utnapishtim,
        who lives so
    free beyond death's deep, deep lake.
        Where can he be?
    Tell me how to venture there where I may learn
        his secrets."
    Finally, Urshanabi uttered these last words
        to Gilgamesh:
    "You yourself have hurt this effort most, sir,
    by blasphemy and sacrilege,
170 by breaking idols and by holding the untouchably
            sacred stones.
    You broke stone images!
    So now, Mr. Gilgamesh, raise high your ax."
    Thus chastised, Gilgamesh
    raised high his ax, unsheathed his sword,
    did penance too as he chopped down many trees;
    prepared them then, and then, brought them
        to Urshanabi.
    After this, they cast off together,
    with push and pull they launched the skiff
180 upon the waving sea.
    They leaped quick, in three short days
    covering a span that any other would
    traverse only after months of passage
    and soon they sailed on to Death's own sea.

Give me another pull, Gilgamesh, upon the mighty oar and then
another...
(figure 30)

Column iv

Still directing the king's new efforts,
  Urshanabi called:
"Give me another pull, Gilgamesh,
  upon the mighty oar
and then another. Give ten times twenty
and then give twenty times ten pulls upon the
mighty oars; then ten more twice; then twice
190 more ten and then confuse the number of
the pulls you put upon the oar
by losing count aloud and starting over."
Halfway through all that pulling,
Gilgamesh had worn the oars to bits
and torn his shirt from off his back
to raise a helping sail upon the mast.
Then Utnapishtim glared down
  from stars and clouds
and mused aloud, as if to coach the world:
"How could any human dare to break the idols
200 or steer the craft that gods and goddesses use?
This stranger is not fit to tie the shoes of servants.
I do see, but I am blind.
I do know, but cannot understand
how he behaves like
the beasts of here and there."

Column v

Gilgamesh spoke many words to Utnapishtim
and told of strife-in-life and
battles rare. He hailed his friend Enkidu,
acclaimed their pride and grieved the
210 death that saddened his great heart.
Gilgamesh raised his prayer

to the remote Utnapishtim:
"Oh myth-filled god,
I have traveled many roads,
crossed many rivers and mountains.
I never rested. I never slept. Grief consumed me.
My clothing was ragged by the time I met
the girl who would help me.
I killed all manner of animal in order
to eat and clothe myself.
220   When I was rejected, I stooped to squalor.
Cursed I went,
being unholy."
Utnapishtim replied:
"Why cry over your fate and nature?
Chance fathered you. Your conception was
an accidental combination
of the divine and mortal.
I do not presume to know how to help
the likes of you."

Column vi

230   Utnapishtim continued:
"No man has ever seen Death.
No one ever heard Death's voice
but Death is real and Death is loud.
How many times must a home be restored
or a contract revised and approved?
How many times must two brothers agree
not to dispute what is theirs?
How many wars and how many floods must there be
with plague and exile in their wake?
240   Shamash is the one who can say.
But there is no one else who can
see what Shamash only can see within the sun.
Behold the cold, cold corpse from a distance,
and then regard the body of one who sleeps.
There seems no difference. How can we say

which is good and which is bad?
And it is also like that with other things as well.
Somewhere above us, where the goddess
   Mammetum decides all things,
Mother Chance sits with the Anunnaki
250 and there she settles all decrees of fable
   and of fortune.
There they issue lengths of lives;
then they issue times of death.
But the last, last matter
is always veiled from human beings.
The length of lives can only be guessed."
Thus spoke Utnapishtim.

THE EPIC OF GILGAMESH

Tablet XI

Columns i - vi

The Flood

Trial of Sleeplessness

Plant of Eternal Life

Foiled by the Serpent

Triumphant Return

Column i

To the most distant and removed of semi-gods,
    to Utnapishtim,
Gilgamesh said:
"When I regard you now, my god-like man,
it's like seeing my own face on calm water
where I dare to study myself.
Like me, you are first of all a fighter
who prefers to war-no-more.
How could one like you, so human, all-too-human,
ascend to be at one with other gods?"

10 Utnapishtim said to him in swift reply:
"Only one as bold as you would dare expect
such knowledge. But I shall tell you what
no person has ever been told.
High up the constant Euphrates
there rests a place you call Shuruppak
where gods and goddesses recline.
Then came the flood, sent by gods' intent.
Mama, Anu, and Enlil were at Shuruppak.
So too was their coachman, Ninurta,

20 and Ennugi, the beastiarius,
and one who watches over precious infants,
  the ever vigilant Ea.
And Ea refrained their chant to the high-grown reeds
upon the shore, giving this advice to me:
'Arise! Arise! Oh wall-like reeds.
Arise and hear my words:
Citizen of Shuruppak, child of Ubaratutu,
abandon your home and build a boat.
Reject the corpse-like stench of wealth.
Choose to live and choose to love;

30 choose to rise above and give back
what you yourself were given.
Be moderate as you flee for survival
in a boat that has no place for riches.
Take the seed of all you need aboard

with you and carefully weigh anchor
after securing a roof that will let in no water.'
Then I said back in reverent prayer:
'I understand, great Ea.
I shall do just as you say to honor god,
40   but for myself
I'll have to find a reason to give the people.'
Then Ea voiced a fair reply:
'Tell those who'll need to know
that Enlil hates you.
Say: "I must flee the city now
and go by sea to where Enlil waits to take my life.
I will descend to the brink of Hell
to be with Ea, god,
who will send riches to you like the rain:
50   all manner of birds;
birds...bords...burds...
and the rarest of rare fish.
The land will fill with crops full grown
    at break of day.
Ea will begin to shower
gifts of life upon you all".'"

Column ii

Then Utnapishtim continued, saying
    words like these:
"By week's end I engineered designs
for an acre's worth of floor upon the ark we built
so that its walls rose straight toward heaven;
60   with decks all round did I design its space;
    120 cubits measured its deck.
With division of six and of seven
I patterned its squares and stairs;
left space for portals too,
secured its beams and stockpiled
all that ever could be used.

Pitch for the hull I poured into the kiln
and ordered three full volumes of oil
to start with and two times three more yet.
For what is security?
70 Each day I sacrificed the holy bulls
and chosen sheep for the people
and pushed the laborers to great fatigue
and thirst, allayed alone by wine
which they drank as if it were water running
from barrels set up for holding cheer
in preparation for a New Year's party they expected.
I set up an ointment box
and cleaned my fingers with its cream.
After one week, the ark was done,
80 though launching was more work than fun
since hull boards caught and snapped
until the water burst most of its great ton.
I supplied the craft with all I owned
of silver, gold, and seed.
My clan brought on the food they'd eat
and all the things we thought we'd need.
At last, it was my turn just then
to shepherd beasts and birds and
babies wet and loud.
90 It was Shamash who ordained the time, saying:
'Prepare the way for your whole boat
and set to sail when the storm
begins to threaten you.'
The Anunnaki too then cried for them.
The gods themselves, finally suffering, sat up
and let their first tears flow down
cheeks and over lips pressed closed.

Column iii

For the whole next week
the sky screamed and storms wrecked the earth
100 and finally broke the war
which groaned as one in labor's throes.
Even Ishtar then bemoaned the
fates of her sad people.
Ocean silent.
Winds dead.
Flood ended.
Then I see a dawn so still;
all humans beaten to dirt
and earth itself like some vast roof.
110 I peeked through the portal into a morning sun
then turned, knelt and cried.
Tears flooded down my face.
Then I searched high and low for the shoreline,
finally spotting an island near and dear.
Our boat stuck fast beside Mt. Nimush.
Mt. Nimush held the hull that could not sway
    for one whole week.
I released the watch-bird, to soar in search of land.
The bird came back within a day
exhausted, unrelieved from lack of rest.
120 I then released a swallow, to soar in search of land.
The bird came back within a day
exhausted, unrelieved from lack of rest.
I then released a raven, to soar in search of land.
The bird took flight above more shallow seas,
found food and found release and found no
need to fly on back to me.
These birds I then released to earth's four corners
and offered sacrifice,
a small libation to the heights of many mountains,
130 from numbered chalices that I arranged.
Under these I spread the scents that gods favored

and when the gods smelled the sweet perfume
　of sacrifice,
they gathered in flight all above, like apparitions.

Column iv

From distant heights with heavenly sights,
the female of all female gods descended then;
Aruru who aroused the wry thought
that Anu made for intercourse.
'Great gods from far and wide
keep always in my mind
140　this thought for intercourse,
tokened by the sacred blue medallion on my neck.
Let me recall with smiles
these days in days to come.
Gods of my shoreline, gods of my sky,
come round this food that I prepared for you;
but do not let Enlil enjoy this too,
since he's the one who drowned my relatives
without telling the gods what he set out to do.'
When Enlil saw the boat, he released
150　his calm reason and let in the Igigi,
　　monsters of blood.
'What force dares defy my anger!?
How dare a man be still alive!?'
Then with these words Ninurta said to Enlil:
'Can any of us besides Ea, maker of words,
create such things as speech?'
Then with these words Ea himself said to Enlil:
'Sly god,
sky darkener,
and tough fighter,
160　how dare you drown so many little people
without consulting me?
Why not just kill the one who offended you,
drown only the sinner?

I ...
...offered sacrifice,
a small libation...
Under these I spread the scents that gods favored
and when the gods smelled the sweet perfume
of sacrifice,
they gathered in flight all above, like apparitions.
(figure 31)

Keep hold of his lifecord; harness his destiny.
Rather than killing rains, set cats at people's throats.
Rather than killing rains, set starvation on dry,
    parched throats.
Rather than killing rains, set sickness on the minds
    and hearts of people.
I was not the one who revealed
    our god-awful secrets.
Blame Utnapishtim, Mr. Know-it-all,
170 who sees everything,
    who knows everything.'
Reflect on these stories, my Gilgamesh.
Then Enlil swooped down around my boat;
he gently raised me from the slime,
placed my wife beside my kneeling form
and blessed us both at once with hands
    upon our bowed heads.
So was it ordained.
So we were ordained."
Earlier than that time, Utnapishtim was not divine.
180 Then with his wife, he was deified
and sent to rule the place where rivers start.
"Gods sent me everywhere to rule the place
    where rivers start.
As for you, Gilgamesh, which gods
    will be called on
to direct your path and future life?
Arise! Be alert! Stay up with stars for
seven long and sleepless nights!"
But even as he tried to stay awake,
fog-like sleep rolled over his eyes.
Then Utnapishtim said these words:
190 "Dear wife, behold the one who tries to pray
while fog-like sleep rolls over his eyes."
She said to him who rarely talks:
"Arouse him now and let him
leave unharmed. Permit that one
to go back home at last."

Column v

Then Utnapishtim said these words:
"An upset soul can upset many gods.
Be kind with food and generous to him.
But keep a count of how he
200　sleeps and what he eats."
She was kind with food and gentle with the man
and she kept count of how he slept.
"One, two, three, alarie,
he slept with death-the-fairy.
Four, five, six, alarie,
he looked so cold and wary."
Then he returned from death to breath!
So Gilgamesh said to the One-who-rarely-spoke:
"Just as I slipped toward sleep,
210　you sent my dream."
And to him in reply, Utnapishtim said these words:
"One, two, three, alarie,
you slept with death-the-fairy.
Four, five, six, alarie,
you looked so cold and wary.
Then you arose from death to breath."
So Gilgamesh said to the One-who-rarely-speaks:
"Help me, Utnapishtim. Where is
home for one like me whose self
220　was robbed of life? My own
bed is where death sleeps and
I crack her spine on every line
where my foot falls."
Utnapishtim calls out to the sailor-god:
"Urshanabi, dear, you will never land
again easily or easily sail the seas
to shores where you no more will find safe harbor.
Sandy and disheveled hair does not become
the one you nearly drowned.
230　Shingles now spoil his hidden beauty.
Better find a place to clean him up.

Better race to pools of saltless water soon
so that by noon he'll shine again for all of us to see.
Tie up his curly hair with ribbon fair.
Place on his shoulders broad the happy robe
so that he may return to his native city easily
   in triumph.
Allow him to wear the sacred elder's cloak
and see that it is always kept
   as clean as it can be."
The sailor-god brought Gilgamesh
240 to where they cleaned his wounds.
By noon he shone again for all to see.
He tied his curly hair with ribbon fair,
and placed upon his shoulder broad the happy robe
so he would return to Uruk easily in triumph
with a cloak unstained and unstainable.
Urshanabi and Gilgamesh launched the boat
over the breakers on the beach and
started to depart across the seas.

Column vi

To her distant husband, Utnapishtim's wife said:
250 "This Gilgamesh has labored much to come here.
Can you reward him for traveling back?"
At that very moment, Gilgamesh used paddles
to return his craft along the shore.
Then Utnapishtim called out to him:
"Gilgamesh! You labored much to come here.
How can I reward you for traveling back?
May I share a special secret, one
that the gods alone do know?
There is a plant that hides somewhere
   among the rocks
260 that thirsts and thrusts itself deep
in the earth, with thistles that sting.
That plant contains eternal life for you."

but in the pool, a cruel snake slithered by
and stole the plant from Gilgamesh
who saw the snake grow young again
(figure 32)

Immediately, Gilgamesh set out in search.
Weighed down carefully, he dove beneath
the cold, cold waters and saw the plant.
Although it stung him when he grabbed its leaf,
he held it fast as he then slipped off his weights
and soared back to the surface.
Then Gilgamesh said this to Urshanabi,
  the sailor-god:
270 "Here is the leaf that begins
all life worth having.
I am bound now for Uruk,
town-so-full-of-shepherds,
and there I'll dare to give
this plant to aged men as food
and they will call it life-giving.
I too intend to eat it
and to be made forever young."
After 10 miles they ate.
280 After 15 miles they set up camp
where Gilgamesh slipped into a pool;
but in the pool, a cruel snake slithered by
and stole the plant from Gilgamesh
who saw the snake grow young again,
as off it raced with the special, special plant.
Right there and then Gilgamesh began to weep
and, between sobs, said to the sailor-god
  who held his hand:
"Why do I bother working for nothing?
Who even notices what I do?
290 I don't value what I did
and now only the snake has
won eternal life. In minutes,
swift currents will lose forever
that special sign that god had left for me."
Then they set out again,
this time upon the land.
After 10 miles they stopped to eat.

After 30 miles they set up camp.
Next day they came to Uruk, full of shepherds.
300   Then Gilgamesh said this to the boatman:
"Rise up now, Urshanabi, and examine
Uruk's wall. Study the base, the brick,
the old design. Is it permanent as can be?
Does it look like wisdom designed it?
The house of Ishtar in
Uruk is divided into three parts:
the town itself, the palm grove, and the prairie."

Place on his shoulders broad the happy robe
so that he may return to his native city
easily in triumph.
(figure 33)

"If only I'd have protected our instruments in
  the safe home of the drum-maker;
If only I'd have given so precious a harp to the
craftsman's wife, she who shepherds such
  jewel-like children.
God, has your heart forgotten me?
Who shall descend to Hell and redeem the
drum from where it rests unused?
Who shall risk his life to retrieve
the precious gifts of Ishtar from death?"

10 And for this quest his friend alone did pledge.
So Gilgamesh said this to Enkidu:
"Descend, descend to Hell where life does end
but listen now to words you need to know.
Go slow to where death rules, my brother dear,
and then arise again above and over fear."
And, once more, Gilgamesh said this to Enkidu:
"Let all who would be saved today, take heed,
and listen to god's words in time of need.
When walking with the strong or with the dead,
20 do not wear clothes of purple or of red.
Shun make-up that presents a holy face
for they attack the phony and the base.
Leave here with me your knife and rock and club;
such weapons only add to their own strife.
Put down your bow, as you would leave a wife.
The souls of death will soil your hands and feet.
Go naked, filthy, tearful, when you meet.
Be quiet, mild, remote, and distant too
as those who will surround and follow you.
30 Greet no girl with kiss so kind upon her lips;
push none away from you with fingertips.
Hold no child's hand as you descend to Hell
and strike no boy who chooses there to dwell.
Around you, Enkidu, the lament of the dead
will whirl and scream,
for she alone, in that good place, is at home who,
having given birth to beauty,

has watched that beauty die.
No graceful robe any longer graces her naked self
40 and her kind breasts, once warm with milk,
have turned into bowls of cold stone."
But Enkidu refused to heed his friend
as he set out that day to then descend
to where the dead who-do-not-live do stay.
He wore bright clothes of celebrative red,
the sight of which offended all the dead.
His colored face made him seem fair and good
but spirits hate the flesh that would dare
remind us of the beauty they have lost.
50 He brought with him his club and rock and knife
and did cause strife with those whom he did mock.
There, too, is where he showed off;
where he went clothed among the naked,
where he wasted food beside the starving,
where he danced beside the grief stricken.
He kissed a happy girl.
He struck a good woman.
He enjoyed his fatherhood.
He fought with his son.
60 Around him, the lament for the dead arose;
for she alone, in that sad place, is at home who,
having given birth to beauty,
has watched that beauty die.
No graceful robe any longer graces her naked self
and her kind breasts, once warm with milk,
have turned into bowls of cold stone.
She never even dreamed once of letting him return
to life. Namtar, the decision-maker,
would not help Enkidu. Nor would illness
70 help. Hell became his home.
Nergal, chief-enforcer, would not help.
Dirges and laments rose all around.
Not even the soldier's death-in-battle,
with all its false and phony honor,
helped Enkidu. Death just

swallowed him, unrecognized.
So the great son of Ninsun, proud Gilgamesh,
cried for his beloved friend
and went to the temple of Enlil,
the savage god of soldiers,

80 to say: "My god, when death
called for me, my best friend went
in my place and he is now no longer living."
But the savage god of soldiers, Enlil, was mute.
So Gilgamesh turned next to one who flies alone,
and to the moon he said: "My god, when death
called for me, my best friend went
in my place and he is now no longer living."
But the moon, who flies alone, was also mute;
so he went next to Ea, whose waters fill

90 the desert oasis even when no rain falls.
"My god," he cried, "when death
called for me, my best friend went
in my place and he is now no longer living."
And Ea, whose waters keep us alive as we journey
    over desert sands,
said this to Nergal, great soldier in arms.
"Go now, mighty follower; free Enkidu to speak
    once to kin
and show this Gilgamesh how to descend halfway
to Hell through the bowels of earth."
And Nergal, accustomed to absurd orders,

100 obeyed as soldiers do.
He freed Enkidu to speak once to kin
and showed Gilgamesh how to descend halfway
to Hell through the bowels of earth.
Enkidu's shadow rose slowly toward the living
and the brothers, tearful and weak,
tried to hug, tried to speak,
tried and failed to do anything but sob.
"Speak to me please, dear brother,"
whispered Gilgamesh.

110 "Tell me of death and where you are."

"Not willingly do I speak of death,"
said Enkidu in slow reply.
"But if you wish to sit for a brief
time, I will describe where I do stay."
"Yes," his brother said in early grief.
"All my skin and all my bones are dead now.
All my skin and all my bones are now dead."
"Oh no," cried Gilgamesh without relief.
"Oh no," sobbed one enclosed by grief.
120 "Did you see there a man who
   never fathered any child?"
"I saw there a no-man who died."
"Did you see there a man whose one son died?"
"I saw him sobbing all alone in open fields."
"Did you see there a man with two grown sons?"
"I did indeed and he smiles all day long."
"Did you see there a man with
   three of his own boys?"
"I did, I did; and his heart's full of joys."
"Did you there see a king with four full kids?"
"I did see one whose pleasure is supreme."
130 "Did you see there anyone with five children?"
"Oh yes, they go about with laughs and shouts."
"And could you find a man with six or seven boys?"
"You could and they are treated as the gods."
"Have you seen one who died too soon?"
"Oh yes; that one sips water fair and rests
each night upon a couch."
"Have you seen one who died in War?"
"Oh yes; his aged father weeps
   and his young widow visits graves."
"Have you seen one buried poor, with other
   homeless nomads?"
140 Oh yes; that one knows rest that is not sure,
far from the proper place."
"Have you seen a brother crying among relatives
who chose to ignore his prayers?"
"Oh yes; he brings bread to the hungry from

the dumps of those who feed their dogs
with food they keep from people
and he eats trash that no other man would want."

GLOSSARY

T he following people, gods, goddesses and places are mentioned in this edition of *The Epic of Gilgamesh*. Since there is no scholarly certainty about the pronunciation of some of the terms, phonetic pronunciations assimilated from various sources are included here. These do not pretend to be the final word — merely a device to help the reader experience a fluid reading, unhampered by the otherwise inevitable stumbling over unfamiliar terms.

Anu (ah' noo) - father of the gods and sky god associated with all heavenly wonder, father of Ishtar. The city of Uruk was sacred to him.

Anunnaki (ah noo nah' kee) - spirit gods of the underworld who judged and determined the fates of the dead.

Aruru (ah roo' roo) - great mother goddess of creation who molds Enkidu from clay in the images of Anu and Ninurta. She is also called Mammetum in her role of decreeing destinies.

Dilmun (deel' moon) - paradise regained, land where the sun rises, where the deified Utnapishtim settled after surviving the great flood.

Ea (ay' ah) - god of water and wisdom, protector of human beings, his breath-born words encourage hope. He is also called Enki.

Eanna (ay ahn' ah) - the sacred temple of Anu and Ishtar in the city of Uruk.

Egalmah (ay' gahl mah) - the sacred temple of Ninsun in the city of Uruk.

Enkidu (en' kee doo) - a "natural" man created by Aruru, modeled after Anu and Ninurta, to become a rival then friend/alter ego to Gilgamesh. He is introduced to civilization by his union with Shamhat, the sacred temple girl.

Enlil (en' lil) - god of earth, wind and air associated with the savage arts of soldiers. He sent the great flood that drowned all but Utnapishtim and his family and sent Humbaba to guard the cedar forest.

Ennugi (en noo' gee) - minor gods or demons

Euphrates (you fray' teez) - river originating in the mountains in the north of Turkey and emptying into the Persian Gulf after joining the Tigris. Ancient Mesopotamia, "The-land-between-two-rivers," derives its name from its location between the Euphrates on the west and the Tigris on the east and is believed to be the cradle of civilization.

Gilgamesh (gil' gah mesh) - hero of the epic, son of the goddess Ninsun and possibly former king of Uruk, Lugalbanda. His insatiable appetites and unbridled behavior drive his subjects to seek help from the gods to divert his overabundant energies from their sons, daughters, and brides. Gilgamesh is an historic figure, as well as the legendary hero of a number of ancient tales.

Humbaba (hoom bah' bah) - nature god, assigned by Enlil to oversee the cedar forest, slain by Gilgamesh and Enkidu. He is also called Huwawa.

Igigi (ee gee' gee) - collective name for the great gods of heaven associated with blood, madness and revenge, often associated with the Anunnaki.

Irkalla (ear kahl' lah) - a name for the underworld, also used in place of Ereshkigal, the queen of the underworld and wife of Nergal.

Ishara (ee shah' rah) - see Ishtar

Ishtar (eesh' tar) - goddess of love and sexuality, also of war, patron of Uruk with her father Anu. She wrought deadly havoc after her rejection by Gilgamesh. She is called Ishara in her role during the sacred ritual of marriage, and is also called Inanna and Irnini.

Ishullanu (ee shoo lah' noo) - gardener of Anu, one of the many discarded lovers of Ishtar.

Lugalbanda (loo gahl bahn' dah) - shepherd and early king of Uruk, thought to be the father of Gilgamesh. He was later deified.

Mt. Mashu (mah' shoo) - twin peaks representing the place where the sun would rise and fall.

Mt. Nimush (nee' moosh) - peak on which Utnapishtim's ark came to rest, formerly called Nisir.

Namtar (nahm' tahr) - underworld demon linked with fate as a negative destiny.

Nergal (near' gahl) - chief god of the underworld responsible for plagues, chief enforcer and soldier-in-arms.

Ninsun (neen' soon) - wise goddess, mother of Gilgamesh, wife of Lugalbanda. Her name means "lady wild cow."

Ninurta (neen oor' tah) - god of war and agriculture, associated with the south wind. Enkidu is created partially in his image.

Nippur (nee poor') - city sacred to Enlil, religious capital of ancient Mesopotamia.

Nisaba (nee sah' bah) - goddess of grain, often depicted with hair of breeze-blown grain. Enkidu's hair resembled hers.

Shamash (shah' mahsh) - sun god and god of justice who despises evil. He encourages Gilgamesh to destroy Humbaba and protects him in the endeavor.

Shamhat (shahm' haht) - sacred girl most likely from the temple of Ishtar who brings civilization to Enkidu through her union with him.

Shuruppak (shoo' roo pahk) - an ancient city of Sumer located north of Uruk, former home of Utnapishtim, from where the gods issued the great flood.

Siduri (see door' ee) - barmaid who lives near the salvific shore. She advises Gilgamesh to abandon his quest for immortality and enjoy the temporal pleasures allotted to mortals while he may.

Sin (seen) - moon god.

Tammuz (tahm' mooz) - shepherd of Uruk, god of vegetation, virgin boy until his union with Ishtar, then another of her discarded lovers. He is also called Dumuzi.

Ubaratutu (oo bahr ah too' too) - god and father of Utnapishtim, former king of Shuruppak.

Ulay (oo lie') - river where Gilgamesh and Enkidu rested.

Urshanabi (oor shah nah' bee) - ferryman and sailor god whose boat crosses the waters separating the garden of the sun from the paradise where the deified Utnapishtim lives. He conveys Gilgamesh to Utnapishtim.

Uruk (oo' rook) - ancient city on the Euphrates River, a center of Sumerian culture circa 3000 B.C., kingdom of Gilgamesh and sacred to Anu and Ishtar.

Utnapishtim (oot nah peesh' teem) - legendary survivor of the great flood who was granted immortality. Gilgamesh seeks from him the secret of eternal life. He is also called Ziusudra.